A LifeGuide  Bible Study

JOHN

The Way to True Life

12 STUDIES IN 2 PARTS
FOR INDIVIDUALS OR GROUPS

Douglas Connelly

With Notes for Leaders

IVP Connect
An imprint of InterVarsity Press
Downers Grove, Illinois

To Jon

InterVarsity Press
P.O. Box 1400, Downers Grove, IL 60515-1426
World Wide Web: www.ivpress.com
E-mail: mail@ivpress.com

©1990, 2002 by Douglas Connelly

InterVarsity Press® is the book-publishing division of InterVarsity Christian Fellowship/USA®, a student movement active on campus at hundreds of universities, colleges and schools of nursing in the United States of America, and a member movement of the International Fellowship of Evangelical Students. For information about local and regional activities, write Public Relations Dept., InterVarsity Christian Fellowship/USA, 6400 Schroeder Rd., P.O. Box 7895, Madison, WI 53707-7895, or visit the IVCF website at <www.intervarsity.org>.

LifeGuide® is a registered trademark of InterVarsity Christian Fellowship.

Cover photograph: Andrew Wenzel/Masterfile

ISBN-10: 0-8308-3006-5
ISBN-13: 978-0-8308-3006-0

Printed in the United States of America ∞

P   23   22   21   20   19   18   17   16   15   14   13
Y   19   18   17   16   15   14   13   12   11   10

Contents

PART 2: JESUS, THE LIVING WAY TO GOD
JOHN 13—21

Getting the Most Out of *John*

The most significant fact in history can be summed up in four words: *Jesus Christ is God!*

The great declaration of the Bible is that God in human flesh was born in Bethlehem. It was God in the person of Jesus Christ who astonished the people of his day with his miracles and amazed them with his teaching. It was God who lived a perfect life and then allowed himself to be put to death on a Roman cross for humanity's sins. It was God who broke the bonds of death three days after he died and came out of the grave alive. The deity of Jesus—the fact that he was God in human form—is the bottom line of the Christian faith.

When the apostle John sat down to write his Gospel, he was not interested simply in adding one more account of Jesus' life to the three already in existence. John wrote his book with a very specific purpose in mind:

> Jesus did many other miraculous signs in the presence of his disciples, which are not recorded in this book. But these are written that you may believe that Jesus is the Christ, the Son of God, and that by believing you may have life in his name. (John 20:30-31)

John's book is not a biography; it's a theological argument. John wants to convince us that Jesus of Nazareth is God the Son. Then he wants to show us how that fact will change our lives in some amazing ways. It is by believing in Jesus Christ as the Son of God that we find life—real life, eternal life, a whole new kind of life!

Every event John records is designed to show us that Jesus is God. John pulls from the life of Jesus specific incidents that demonstrate his majesty and deity. Of particular interest to John are the sign miracles of Jesus. In the first twelve chapters of his book he records seven miracles. These miracles were not performed simply to relieve human suffering or to meet human needs; they were "signs." They pointed to the truth of Jesus' claim to be the Son of God.

John was the last Gospel writer. The best evidence points to a date around A.D. 90 for the composition of his Gospel. The other Gospels had been in circulation for some time. John wrote to add his unique perspective and to fill in some of the details not recorded by the other writers. He assumes his readers are familiar with the other Gospels. John does not mention, for example, the anguish of Jesus in the Garden of Gethsemane. The other writers had adequately described that incident. John does, however, give us the details of Jesus' conversation with his disciples on the night before his crucifixion. The other writers mention it only briefly.

John never mentions himself by name in the Gospel; he refers to himself simply as "the disciple whom Jesus loved." We have in this Gospel the memories of an intimate friend about Jesus. Jesus had transformed John's life. I hope you are prepared to have that happen to you! You are about to begin a fascinating study focused on the greatest person who ever lived—Jesus Christ. If you will respond to what John writes in faith and obedience, you, like John, will experience a whole new kind of life.

Suggestions for Individual Study

1. As you begin each study, pray that God will speak to you through his Word.

2. Read the introduction to the study and respond to the personal reflection question or exercise. This is designed to help you focus on God and on the theme of the study.

3. Each study deals with a particular passage—so that you can delve into the author's meaning in that context. Read and reread the passage to be studied. The questions are written using the language of the New International Version, so you may wish to use that version of the Bible. The New Revised Standard Version is also recommended.

4. This is an inductive Bible study, designed to help you discover for yourself what Scripture is saying. The study includes three types of questions. *Observation* questions ask about the basic facts: who, what, when, where and how. *Interpretation* questions delve into the meaning of the passage. *Application* questions help you discover the implications of the text for growing in Christ. These three keys unlock the treasures of Scripture.

Write your answers to the questions in the spaces provided or in a personal journal. Writing can bring clarity and deeper understanding of yourself and of God's Word.

5. It might be good to have a Bible dictionary handy. Use it to look up any unfamiliar words, names or places.

6. Use the prayer suggestion to guide you in thanking God for what you have learned and to pray about the applications that have come to mind.

7. You may want to go on to the suggestion under "Now or Later," or you may want to use that idea for your next study.

Suggestions for Members of a Group Study

1. Come to the study prepared. Follow the suggestions for individual study mentioned above. You will find that careful preparation will greatly enrich your time spent in group discussion.

2. Be willing to participate in the discussion. The leader of your group will not be lecturing. Instead, he or she will be encouraging the members of the group to discuss what they have learned. The leader will be asking the questions that are found in this guide.

3. Stick to the topic being discussed. Your answers should be based on the verses which are the focus of the discussion and not on outside authorities such as commentaries or speakers. These studies focus on a particular passage of Scripture. Only rarely should you refer to other portions of the Bible. This allows for everyone to participate in in-depth study on equal ground.

4. Be sensitive to the other members of the group. Listen attentively when they describe what they have learned. You may be surprised by their insights! Each question assumes a variety of answers. Many questions do not have "right" answers, particularly questions that aim at meaning or application. Instead the questions push us to explore the passage more thoroughly.

When possible, link what you say to the comments of others. Also, be affirming whenever you can. This will encourage some of the more hesitant members of the group to participate.

5. Be careful not to dominate the discussion. We are sometimes so eager to express our thoughts that we leave too little opportunity for others to respond. By all means participate! But allow others to also.

6. Expect God to teach you through the passage being discussed and through the other members of the group. Pray that you will have an enjoyable and profitable time together, but also that as a result of the study you will find ways that you can take action individually and/or as a group.

7. Remember that anything said in the group is considered confidential and should not be discussed outside the group unless specific permission is given to do so.

8. If you are the group leader, you will find additional suggestions at the back of the guide.

1

Encountering the Word

John 1

It was a great day in our history when a man first walked on the moon. But the Bible declares that a far greater event took place two thousand years ago: God walked on the earth. God the Son, Jesus Christ, came to live among us as a real human being.

GROUP DISCUSSION. What famous person alive today would you like to spend a day with? Why?

PERSONAL REFLECTION. What do you hope will happen in your life as a result of studying the Gospel of John?

John opens his Gospel with a beautiful hymn of exaltation to Christ. It is one of the most profound passages in the whole Bible. It is written in simple, direct language, but the truth it contains has never been fully explained. We come upon an ocean-sized truth but have to be content to paddle around in shallow water. *Read John 1:1-18.*

1. Why do you think John calls Jesus "the Word" (vv. 1, 14)?

2. In verses 1-5 what facts does John declare to be true of the Word?

Which of these facts most helps you understand who Jesus is?

---

3. John contrasts Jesus' rejection by the majority with his reception by a few (vv. 9-13). What truths about Jesus should have brought the majority to receive him (vv. 9-11)?

---

4. How would you explain to someone both the meaning and the results of receiving Jesus (vv. 12-13)?

---

5. According to verses 14-18, what specific aspects of God's character are revealed to us through Jesus?

---

6. *Read John 1:19-34.* In verses 8 and 9 and again in these verses another John is introduced. He is not the author of the Gospel but John the Baptizer, Jesus' relative, and the one who announced Jesus' coming to the people of his day. What steps does John the Baptist take to guarantee that people will not look at him but at Jesus?

---

7. How would you summarize John the Baptist's testimony concerning Jesus?

8. *Read John 1:35-51.* In these verses we are introduced to five men: Andrew, Simon, Philip, Nathanael and one unnamed disciple (John). How does each man respond to the testimony he hears about Jesus?

9. Which of these responses have you encountered as you have shared your faith in Jesus Christ?

10. What would you be most interested in investigating about Jesus if you could go back in time to the events in this chapter?

11. John records more than a dozen names or descriptions of Jesus in this chapter. Which of the names of Jesus has the most significance to you personally? Explain why.

Thank Jesus for coming to explain God fully to us. Use some of the titles and descriptions from this chapter to express your worship and praise to him.

Now or Later

Consider some ways that you (as an individual or as a group) can be a witness for Jesus in your community. Plan to take one specific action this week to demonstrate Jesus' love to others who don't yet know him.

2

Signs of God

After I had given a presentation on the claims of Jesus, a skeptical student asked, "What proof do you have that Jesus really was who he claimed to be?" People have been asking that question for two thousand years! For John the convincing proof of Jesus' deity was found in his words and deeds. No one but God could say the things Jesus said, and no one but God could do the things Jesus did.

GROUP DISCUSSION. What miracle or achievement would you choose to launch yourself into a political campaign or into public ministry? What effect do you think it would have?

PERSONAL REFLECTION. What initially convinced you that Jesus was more than a man?

In chapter 2 John pulls two events from the early ministry of Jesus that demonstrate his power and authority. We are shown a miraculous sign as Jesus exercises his creative power to turn water into wine. We are also shown a sign of Jesus' authority as he cleanses God's temple in Jerusalem. Both signs demonstrate that Jesus was the fullness of God clothed in humanity. *Read John 2:1-11.*

1. If you had been a wedding guest, what do you imagine your reaction would have been to this miracle?

2. When the groom's parents run out of wine for their guests, Jesus' mother asks him to help (v. 3). What do you think Mary expects Jesus to do? (Remember, according to verse 11, Jesus had not performed any miracles.)

3. What does Jesus mean by his reply to Mary in verse 4?

4. According to verse 11, the purpose of Jesus' miracle is not to save the groom from embarrassment but to display Jesus' glory. What aspects of Christ's glory does this miracle reveal to you?

5. What area of your life seems like plain water right now?

How could Jesus transform that problem or relationship?

6. *Read John 2:12-25.* How does John's picture of Jesus in verses 15-16 fit with today's popular concept of him?

7. What is the significance of Jesus' claim that the temple is "my Father's house" (v. 16)?

8. Only the Messiah, God's promised deliverer, has the authority to cleanse the temple. The people recognize that fact and ask Jesus for a miraculous sign to confirm his identity (v. 18). How would the sign

Jesus points to be particularly meaningful to them (vv. 19-22)?

9. Why don't the disciples immediately grasp what Jesus is talking about when he says, "Destroy this temple, and I will raise it again in three days" (vv. 19, 22)?

10. If people were believing in Jesus because of the miraculous signs, why doesn't Jesus "entrust himself to them" (vv. 23-25)?

11. What does this passage reveal about Jesus' concern for his Father's reputation?

12. In what practical ways can you demonstrate in your life the same concern for the holy character of God?

Express your openness to Jesus' authority in your life and heart. Give him permission to drive out whatever dishonors him. Ask him to change the stagnant water of your life into vibrant wine.

Now or Later

Think about what aspects of your life Jesus may want to clean up or change—work or school habits, your words, your thought life, a relationship, your entertainment preferences. Would you welcome Jesus into those areas, or would you question his right to intrude?

3

Starting Over

I recently talked to a junior in college who is only one month old. No, she isn't a child genius. A few weeks ago a friend explained to her who Jesus is and how much Jesus loved her. As she responded in simple faith, she experienced the joy of spiritual birth.

GROUP DISCUSSION. What's the best gift you have ever received? Why was it so special?

PERSONAL REFLECTION. What would you do differently if you could start life over again?

"Born again" is a phrase used in our culture for everything from skin cream to surfboards. It surprises some people to learn that the original trademark for that expression came from Jesus. He used it to bring a very religious man to a life-changing decision. *Read John 3.*

1. How would you describe Nicodemus to a friend? What kind of person was he?

2. Jesus' reply to Nicodemus in verse 3 seems to have nothing to do with Nicodemus's statement in verse 2. Why do you think Jesus brings up the subject of new birth?

3. Why does Nicodemus respond to Jesus' explanation with such amazement (v. 9)?

4. Why is Jesus likewise amazed at Nicodemus's ignorance (vv. 10-12)?

5. How does the story of Moses lifting up the snake in the desert illustrate our need and Christ's offer of salvation (vv. 14-15; see Numbers 21:4-9)?

6. What impresses you about God in verses 16 and 17?

7. What do you learn about yourself (as part of "the world") in those verses?

8. Verses 18 through 21 emphasize the importance of our personal response to Jesus Christ. How would you describe your response to him?

9. In your opinion, what motivates John the Baptist's disciples to raise the issue of Jesus' ministry (vv. 22-26)?

---

10. How would you summarize John's view of the character and ministry of Jesus (vv. 27-36)?

---

11. What are some ways you can demonstrate Jesus' superiority over all that you are and all that you own?

Ask God to prepare you to speak confidently to others about the role of Jesus in your life.

Now or Later

Think about a person you know who needs to hear the truth about Jesus. Plan to spend some time with that person, and look for opportunities to tell them about Jesus and how he has changed your life.

4

Connecting with People

John 4

Think of the people you least want to be around—crooked politicians, racial bigots, violent gang members or drug dealers. We don't talk to some people about Jesus out of fear or because we think they won't want to listen. People in Jesus' day had the same fears and prejudices. Jesus, however, broke through any barrier if it meant bringing a person to faith.

GROUP DISCUSSION. When have you been able to turn an ordinary conversation into a discussion about Jesus?

PERSONAL REFLECTION. Who are you afraid or reluctant to talk with about Jesus? What factors make you hesitant?

In John 4 we see Jesus reach out first to a woman, then to his disciples and finally to a grieving father. Watching Jesus give himself to people with love and compassion will help us care for those God puts in our paths. *Read John 4:1-26.*

1. Why do you think Jesus "had to go through Samaria" on his way to

Galilee (v. 4)? (Jewish people normally went around Samaria to avoid contact with the despised Samaritans.)

2. Jesus' words surprise the Samaritan woman (v. 9). What present-day situations might arouse the same racial, religious and sexual prejudices?

3. How does Jesus' offer of "living water" contrast with what the woman thinks he means (vv. 10-15)?

What does this offer of "living water" mean in your life and experience?

4. Why do you think Jesus brings up the woman's long list of past marriages and her present adulterous relationship (vv. 16-18)?

5. How does Jesus respond when the woman suddenly changes the subject and begins talking about the controversy over the proper place of worship (vv. 19-24)?

6. What principles can you draw from Jesus' conversation with the woman to help you in discussing the gospel with non-Christians?

7. *Read John 4:27-54.* How is the disciples' confusion about food (vv. 31-33) similar to the woman's confusion about living water?

8. After his encounter with the Samaritan woman, what specific lessons does Jesus apply to his disciples and to us (vv. 34-38)?

9. How does the royal official's attitude differ from the response Jesus had anticipated (v. 44)?

10. What has Jesus taught you in this chapter about your sensitivity and response to people around you who are in need?

How could you reach out to someone who has been rejected by the world and offer Jesus' love?

Identify any obstacles in your mind and heart that keep you from seeing people as God sees them. Give your fears and prejudices to the Lord.

Now or Later

Who were the people responsible for telling you about Jesus? Let them know in a letter or phone call how much you appreciate their concern for you.

What individuals have you had a part in leading to faith in Christ? Let them know in a personal way of your continued concern for their spiritual growth.

5

Deity on Trial

In my high school years I was hooked on lawyer television programs. Those intrepid men and women always found the missing piece of evidence that would rescue the innocent and convict the guilty. I've learned since my high school days that sometimes judges and juries are wrong. Men and women may hear all the evidence and still make a wrong decision.

GROUP DISCUSSION. What are some reasons why people do not believe in or follow Jesus?

PERSONAL REFLECTION. What factors (people, circumstances) helped to bring you to faith in Christ? What factors worked against your belief?

In John 5 Jesus is on trial. It is not a formal trial in a courtroom, but all the elements of a trial appear in the story. A group of people is forced to make a decision about Jesus in their hearts. They hear all the evidence but make a disastrously wrong decision. *Read John 5:1-15.*

1. Picture yourself in the setting of this story. What noises would you

hear? What would you smell? How would you feel being there?

2. What was the disabled man's attitude before his healing, and how did it change?

3. The fourth commandment says, "Remember the Sabbath day by keeping it holy" (see Exodus 20:8-11). In their zeal to apply this command, what do these critics of Jesus fail to see (vv. 9-15)?

4. In what ways has Jesus made you well and whole?

5. *Read John 5:16-47.* Jesus explains that the work of *creation* ended on the seventh day, but not the work of *compassion* (vv. 16-18). Why does his explanation make his enemies even more determined to kill him?

6. What insights do verses 19-23 give us into the Father's devotion to the Son?

the Son's dependence on the Father?

7. According to Jesus, why is our response to him a matter of eternal life or death (vv. 24-30)?

---

8. What "witnesses" does Jesus call forward to testify on his behalf, and how does their testimony validate his claims (vv. 31-40)?

---

9. In verses 39-47 Jesus claims that both the Scriptures and the testimony of Moses stand against his accusers. These religious leaders rested their hope of acceptance before God on their obedience to the written law of Moses. If you were in that situation, would Jesus' challenge make you angry, or would it force you to reevaluate your attitude toward Jesus? Explain your answer.

---

10. What steps can you take to avoid slipping into the kind of religion that is outwardly pious but inwardly bankrupt?

---

11. According to this chapter, what factors influence our verdict for or against Jesus?

Commit yourself in prayer to a growing relationship with the Lord instead of reliance on religious rules.

Now or Later
This week visit a place marked by loneliness or suffering—a hospital, a homeless shelter, a foster-care facility, a prison. Go with a willingness to demonstrate the love of Christ. Be sensitive to the Holy Spirit's direction toward an individual in need.

6

Jesus,
the Bread of Life

John 6

I teach a class for Spring Arbor University, and I see all kinds of responses to pressure. When an assignment is due or the deadline for a paper looms, some people are motivated by that pressure to get the job done. Other people have learned to start early on a project because when the pressure builds they feel paralyzed. Still other students call me in tears, pleading for more time to finish the work. Eventually they discover some ways of coping are more effective than others!

GROUP DISCUSSION. How do you usually respond to an "impossible" situation—a problem in your life that doesn't seem to have a solution?

PERSONAL REFLECTION. Recall a time when you (or a friend) faced circumstances that seemed beyond your ability to handle. How did God demonstrate his presence and power in that situation?

Jesus used just about every life situation to strengthen the faith of his disciples. On this particular day Jesus was faced with a huge crowd of hungry people. Jesus offered them food that would satisfy their spiritual hunger forever. *Read John 6:1-15.*

1. How would you characterize Philip and Andrew's responses to the problem of feeding this enormous crowd (vv. 5-9)?

2. If Jesus knew what he was going to do (v. 6), why do you think he asks these two disciples for advice?

3. How do you think the disciples feel as they gather up the leftover pieces (vv. 12-13)?

4. What insights does this passage give you into how Jesus may be at work in the difficult situations of your life?

5. *Read John 6:16-59.* Imagine that you are one of the disciples, rowing the boat in the dark, rough water (vv. 16-21). How would your perception of Jesus be altered by seeing him walk on water?

6. The next day the people are hungry again, so they come seeking Jesus (vv. 22-25). How does he try to redirect their thinking (vv. 26-33)?

7. Jesus claims to be the bread of life (v. 35). Based on the remarks of some in the crowd (vv. 41-42), do you think they understand what Jesus is saying? Why or why not?

8. When Jesus says, "This bread is my flesh," the crowd thinks only of cannibalism (v. 52). What do you think it means to eat Jesus' flesh and drink his blood (vv. 53-59)?

Is this something we do once for all time, or is it an ongoing process? Explain.

9. *Read John 6:60-71.* Jesus turns away from the crowd and focuses on his disciples. How would you describe their responses to his "hard teaching"?

Which response best describes your present attitude toward Jesus, and why did you choose that answer?

10. Jesus has contrasted the two appetites found in every person—the appetite for food that perishes and the appetite for food that endures. In what way has Jesus satisfied the spiritual hunger in your heart?

Thank God for satisfying all your needs—physical, emotional and spiritual. Be specific in your thanksgiving.

Now or Later

Evaluate how you use your resources of time, money and energy. Based on how you distribute your resources, what needs in your life do you work hardest at meeting? What steps can you take to bring more balance in your life? Ask a friend to hold you accountable for the changes that need to be made.

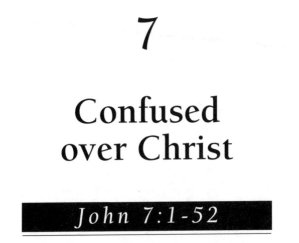

7

Confused
over Christ

John 7:1-52

Not long ago I had a series of conversations with a young man about Jesus Christ and why faith in him is so important. At first, the man was interested. He was open to listening to God's Word and considering Christ's claims. As time went on, however, he became more and more hostile. Finally, he told me that he didn't want to pursue his investigation any further. He had decided to reject Christ and his offer of salvation.

GROUP DISCUSSION. Have you ever had to work with someone who disliked or even hated you? What was it like to face that person every day? (Or what do you think it would be like?)

PERSONAL REFLECTION. How would you feel if a family member or close friend openly doubted your abilities or decisions?

John's Gospel seems to follow the pattern of my conversations with the young man. In the early chapters men and women responded to Jesus with belief. Then some of those who follow him turned away. Now open warfare breaks out between Jesus and his enemies—and yet some still see the truth. *Read John 7:1-13.*

1. The first blast of hostility against Jesus comes from his own family. How would you characterize the statements made by Jesus' brothers?

2. Why do you think Jesus waits to go to Jerusalem until after his brothers have left (v. 10)?

3. What counsel would you give a believer who faces spiritual opposition from his or her family?

4. *Read John 7:14-52.* When Jesus makes his presence in Jerusalem known, people begin to challenge the origin (and, therefore, the authority) of his teaching. According to Jesus, how can we verify the truth of his teaching (vv. 16-18)?

5. What other opinions or questions do people have about Jesus in verses 20-36?

How does Jesus respond to each one?

6. On the last day of the Feast of Tabernacles, large vats of water were poured out on the pavement of the temple court as a reminder of God's provision of water in the wilderness. With that custom in mind, how would you explain the significance of Jesus' remarks in verses 37-39?

To what extent has Christ been a continual source of spiritual refreshment for you?

_____

7. Throughout the chapter John gives us a sampling of various reactions to Jesus. Identify some of the reactions of various people and explain why you think they reacted the way they did.

_____

8. Which of the opinions you have identified in this chapter are still expressed today, and in what way?

_____

9. Based on Jesus' example, what should our response be to such opinions about and reactions toward Jesus?

Sit or kneel quietly before the Lord, and let him bring the refreshment of living water to your heart and mind.

Now or Later
Jesus talks about the Holy Spirit several times in the Gospel of John. If you have access to a Bible concordance, look up the word *Spirit* and read each reference in John. Summarize what each passage teaches about the Spirit's ministry. Here are a few passages to get you started: John 3:5-8; 6:63; 14:25-27; 16:12-14.

8

Caught in Adultery

John 7:53—8:11

Nothing is more humiliating than being caught in an act of disobedience! Whether it's a child with his hand in the cookie jar or an adult driving over the speed limit, we all know the sinking feeling of being caught. We also know the desperation of wanting to be forgiven.

GROUP DISCUSSION. Which is harder for you: to forgive or to seek forgiveness? Why?

PERSONAL REFLECTION. Think of a time when you hurt someone and that person was willing to forgive you. How did it feel to be forgiven?

In John 8 a woman is caught in the most awkward of situations—the very act of adultery. The way Jesus responds to her may surprise you. *Read John 7:53—8:11.*

1. Unlock some of the emotional background of this encounter. How do you think the woman feels when she is publicly accused?

What emotions grip the woman's accusers?

2. What would you have done if you had been part of the crowd that looked on?

3. How do you feel when someone exposes a sin or failure in your life?

4. While it is obvious that the woman is guilty, what elements of a setup can you find in this situation?

5. In your opinion, what does Jesus write in the dirt?

6. The Pharisees and teachers boasted loudly about how good and holy they were. Why do you think they leave rather than stone the woman (vv. 7-9)?

7. How would you describe Jesus' attitude toward the woman (vv. 10-11)?

8. Do you think Jesus is condoning the woman's sin by not condemning her? Explain.

9. If you were the woman, how would you feel as you left Jesus' presence?

10. How do you usually respond when you fail?

11. What can we learn from this passage about Jesus' attitude toward us, even when we feel awful about ourselves?

12. What does this account teach us about forgiving and accepting others?

Thank God for his willingness to forgive you. Ask him to cultivate a spirit of forgiveness in your relationships with others.

Now or Later
Focus on someone you need to forgive or from whom you need to seek forgiveness. Plan a strategy to approach that person with grace and humility. Ask someone older or wiser in the Lord to give you some guidance and to pray for your endeavor to resolve a difficult situation.

9

Shine, Jesus, Shine

Jesus never spoke in public without creating controversy. In fact, he was constantly in trouble! Rather than retreating behind the safety of a pulpit, Jesus spoke in settings where people were bold enough to talk back.

GROUP DISCUSSION. What is your typical response to the promises of a politician or the claims of an advertisement? Are you generally suspicious, or do you tend to be more trusting?

PERSONAL REFLECTION. Have you ever tried to talk about Christ with a family member or coworker who was hostile to your message? How did you feel at the time? How did you try to penetrate that person's spiritual barriers?

In this portion of John's story Jesus makes a series of claims about himself. Each claim is met by a challenge from his enemies. Each challenge is then answered, and the answer leads to the next claim. Throughout this interchange, Jesus shows us how to speak the truth in the face of hostility. He also reveals some amazing things about himself. *Read John 8:12-30.*

---

1. Jesus' first claim is "I am the light of the world. Whoever follows me will never walk in darkness, but will have the light of life." What does it mean to walk in the darkness (v. 12)?

How has following Jesus brought light into your life?

---

2. The Pharisees challenge the validity of Jesus' claim (v. 13; see Deuteronomy 19:15). How does Jesus answer their challenge (vv. 14-18)?

---

3. Jesus' reference to his Father leads to his second claim—that he came from God. In what way does this claim heighten the tension between Jesus and his opponents (vv. 19-30)?

---

4. Jesus says, "If you do not believe that I am the one I claim to be, you will indeed die in your sins" (v. 24). What is the response of our contemporary culture to that claim?

---

5. *Read John 8:31-59.* Jesus makes another startling claim in verses 31-32: "If you hold to my teaching . . . then you will know the truth, and the truth will set you free." Those who hear Jesus' claim interrupt him to say that they are already free. What analysis does Jesus give of their "freedom" (vv. 34-36)?

---

6. Jesus' opponents also claim to have both Abraham and God as their father. According to Jesus, how does their conduct contradict their claim (vv. 39-47)?

7. Why is our conduct the truest test of our beliefs?

8. What is it about Jesus' statements that makes his enemies want to stone him (vv. 48-59)?

9. Summarize the various attacks voiced against Jesus in this chapter, and explain how Jesus' example will help you face spiritually hostile people.

10. In what ways does your lifestyle validate (or invalidate) your claim to be a follower of Jesus?

Let God speak to you about any areas of your life that don't match up with your claim to be his disciple.

Now or Later
If you know someone who is hostile to the message of the gospel, challenge that person to read a book about the Christian faith and then discuss it with you. C. S. Lewis's *Mere Christianity* or John Stott's *Basic Christianity* might be good ones to start with. Listen carefully to your friend's objections, and try to respond openly and courageously. Reading good books on Christian belief will also strengthen your ability to answer those who raise objections to Jesus and his claims.

10

A Blind Man
Sees the Light

John 9

Our sight is a wonderful gift from God. We marvel at the fiery colors of a sunset, the rich pastels of spring and the delicate beauty of a flower. How tragic it must be to never see the light of day.

But there is a far greater tragedy than physical blindness. Some people with twenty-twenty vision are blind spiritually to God and to his work all around them.

GROUP DISCUSSION. Describe your most vivid childhood memory involving darkness. What feelings come over you in the dark?

PERSONAL REFLECTION. In what ways would being blind change your life?

In John 9 Jesus meets a man who has been blind from birth. The man illustrates that those who are blind often see clearly, while others with sight see nothing at all. *Read John 9:1-12.*

1. Based on the question the disciples ask Jesus in verse 2, how do they view the relation between sickness and sin?

What is Jesus' view of the same issue?

---

2. In your opinion, which of these views is more widely held among Christians today? Explain.

---

3. In verse 5 Jesus claims to be the light of the world. In what sense does the physical healing of the blind man confirm Jesus' spiritual claim?

---

4. Why do you think Jesus goes through the process of making mud and instructing the man to go wash, instead of simply healing him instantly?

---

5. *Read John 9:13-41.* How would you describe the initial response to the healed blind man of his neighbors (vv. 8-12)?

of the Pharisees (vv. 13-17)?

of his parents (vv. 18-23)?

of the man himself (vv. 24-34)?

6. On what grounds do the Pharisees object to this miracle (vv. 16, 22, 24, 29)?

7. How do the Pharisees react when the genuineness of the miracle becomes undeniable (vv. 28-34)?

8. When might Christians today exhibit the Pharisees' attitude toward a marvelous work of God's grace or power?

9. What is Jesus' purpose in seeking out the healed man a second time (vv. 35-38)?

10. Through what weakness, failed relationship or disability in your life could God demonstrate his glory?

Thank Jesus for bringing spiritual sight to you.

Now or Later

The blind man believed in Jesus and worshiped him (John 9:38). What do you think the man's worship involved? What posture before Jesus did he take? What words did he say? How can you demonstrate a worshipful attitude toward Jesus?

11

Listening for the Shepherd's Voice

John 10

Sheep are not particularly bright animals. They can't fend for themselves very well. Food and water may be within sight, but they won't go to it unless a shepherd leads them. Sheep get lost easily too, so they need a shepherd to guide them. Sheep can't defend themselves. They have no sharp claws or teeth or wings to fly. Sheep are an easy target for an enemy—unless they have a shepherd to protect them.

It's not much of a compliment when Jesus calls us his sheep. The term wasn't designed to exalt us; it was designed to exalt our shepherd.

GROUP DISCUSSION. What person or trend did you (or your friends) follow when you were teenagers? Why did you follow, and what responses did you receive from others?

PERSONAL REFLECTION. In what situations do you feel most insecure or afraid? How does it help when someone faces those situations with you?

In John 10 Jesus uses the scene of a shepherd enclosing his sheep in a sheepfold to give us one of the most moving pictures of our salvation and assurance in Christ found anywhere in the Bible. If you've ever doubted the love of Christ, Jesus will give you a healthy dose of confidence in this chapter. *Read John 10:1-21.*

1. As you read back through this passage again, identify who or what these images represent, and list the characteristics of each.

The sheep pen:

The shepherd:

The thief:

The sheep:

The gate:

The hired hand:

---

2. In verses 11-15 Jesus talks about the shepherd's care for his sheep. What can you learn from those verses about Jesus' care and relationship with you?

---

3. What does Jesus reveal about the future of his flock (v. 16)? In what ways do you feel a part of "one flock" under "one shepherd"?

---

4. Why do you think Jesus stresses that he lays down his life of his own accord (vv. 17-18)?

---

5. *Read John 10:22-42.* According to Jesus, how are his enemies in this passage different from his sheep (vv. 22-27)?

6. What does Jesus mean when he says, "My sheep listen to my voice . . . and they follow me" (v. 27)?

_____

7. How do you respond to the promises and assurances Jesus gives his sheep in verses 28-29?

_____

8. When Jesus claims that he and the Father are one, the Jews pick up stones to stone him (vv. 30-33). Do you think his defense is a denial of his deity (vv. 33-36)? Explain.

_____

9. What usually prompts you to have doubts about your salvation or your relationship with Jesus: personal failures? feelings of unworthiness? judgment from others? Explain your answer.

_____

10. How will the promises Jesus makes in these verses help you when you struggle with doubt?

Ask the Holy Spirit to fill your heart with confidence in Jesus' promises to you.

Now or Later

The image of God as a shepherd is used many times in the Bible to picture God's care for his people. Read through the following passages and filter out one promise that you can use to strengthen your own faith or to encourage another Christian who may be struggling.

Psalm 23

Psalm 95

Isaiah 40:11

Isaiah 53:6

12

Back from the Dead!

I was murdered in a high school play—stabbed in the back by a treacherous friend. But the next day I was sitting in class as if nothing had happened! No one was shocked to see me alive because my "death" was a deception.

The real experience of death is far more difficult to handle. Ever since God judged Adam and Eve for their sin, death has plagued humanity. It snatches those we love and looms over all our lives like a menacing spirit. The Bible calls death our final enemy.

GROUP DISCUSSION. Think back to the death of a family member or friend. Did that death cause you to question God's love? Explain your answer.

PERSONAL REFLECTION. What feelings do you have when you think about death? What facts about death (if you knew for sure they were true) would ease your concerns?

In this chapter Jesus reaches out to a family struggling with the pain of death. He shows us why we need never fear death again. *Read John 11:1-44.*

1. From the clues in this chapter, describe Jesus' relationship with each member of this family: Mary, Martha and Lazarus.

2. How can we resolve the seeming conflict between Jesus' love for Lazarus and his deliberate delay in helping him (vv. 4-5, 15)?

3. What elements of doubt and faith do you see in Martha's statements to Jesus (vv. 17-27)?

How does Jesus stretch Martha's faith in this brief encounter?

4. Jesus declares to Martha that "he who believes in me will live, even though he dies; and whoever lives and believes in me will never die" (vv. 25-26). What kind of "life" and "death" is Jesus referring to in each case?

5. How does Jesus' statement alter our normal view of life and death?

6. Why do you think John emphasizes that Jesus is deeply moved by Mary's grief and the anguish of those with her (vv. 28-38)?

7. Based on this passage, how would you respond to those who think that grief at a loved one's death is incompatible with real faith?

_____

8. *Read John 11:45-57.* How would you explain the fact that the people who saw the same miracle responded in two totally different ways?

_____

9. What does this account reveal about the value of miracles alone for bringing people to faith in Christ?

_____

10. In what ways will this chapter change the way you respond to personal difficulty or the apparent delay of God?

How will it change the way you pray for those who are going through difficult situations?

Talk to God about how you feel when he seems far away or unconcerned about you. Thank him that he never abandons you as his child.

Now or Later

Focus on a specific situation in your life or in a friend's life that you need to trust God to work out. Write the need on a card or in your journal, and begin to pray about it. Keep a record of how God works.

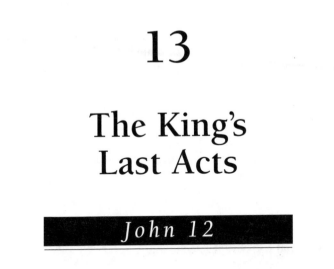

13

The King's Last Acts

John 12

I have a friend who takes the Bible's challenge to "number our days" very literally. He has calculated his expected life span, translated it into days, and he writes the days he has left to live above every day in his planner. Instead of being a morbid reminder of his death, it motivates him to leave a legacy of love and holy living.

GROUP DISCUSSION. If you knew for sure that you had only one week to live, what would you do with that week?

PERSONAL REFLECTION. What acts do you want to be remembered for? How consistently do you do what you want the people you love to remember?

If you have ever felt rejected or misunderstood, you know how Jesus feels as his public ministry comes to an end. The hostility against him has risen to a fever pitch. His gentle compassion and abundant miracles have been met with opposition and violence. Jesus knows what none of his friends know—that he is about to die. In spite of the fleeting attempts of the crowd to make him king, Jesus chooses the way of the cross. *Read John 12:1-11.*

1. Which person in this passage do you identify most closely with: Mary, who loved giving; Jesus, who appreciated receiving; or Judas, who looked only at the cost? Explain why you identify with that person.

2. Judas objects to Mary's extravagance. What motives and wrong thinking lie behind his objection (vv. 4-8)?

3. How would you have reacted to Mary's act?

What can we expect if we are extravagant in our devotion to Jesus?

4. *Read John 12:12-36.* What do the shouts of the crowd tell us about their expectations of Jesus (vv. 12-19)?

5. How do Jesus' statements about his mission clash with the crowd's expectations (vv. 23-28)?

6. Jesus often uses apparent contradictions to drive home a truth. How would you explain verse 25 in terms that apply to your life (see also vv. 26-28)?

7. Jesus makes it clear that he is about to die. What will Jesus' death accomplish (vv. 23-24, 28, 31-32)?

Which of these results is most encouraging to you? Explain why.

8. *Read John 12:37-50.* When we stubbornly refuse to believe, what happens to our spiritual senses, and why (vv. 37-41)?

9. Jesus' last public message to his people is recorded in verses 44-50. What indications do you find that he is still reaching out in love and grace to those who have rejected him?

10. How can you apply the example of Jesus to people who reject you or your witness about Christ?

Reflect on Jesus' commitment to do the Father's will. Prayerfully examine your own direction and life goals in that light.

Now or Later
Jesus refers to our spiritual enemy, Satan, as "the prince of this world" in John 12:31. Earlier Jesus called him a murderer and the father of lies (John 8:44). In what way has Jesus' death on the cross "driven out" Satan? What resources are available to you when you are under attack spiritually?

14

The Son
as a Slave

There were two things on Jesus' heart the night before his crucifixion—his Father and his disciples. In chapters 13—17 of John we have the privilege of listening to his conversations with them both. Before Jesus can instruct his disciples about his death, however, he has to act out a lesson in servitude.

GROUP DISCUSSION. Have you ever been asked to do a demeaning, lowly job? What thoughts went through your mind at that time?

PERSONAL REFLECTION. Do you feel awkward or uncomfortable when others try to serve you? Why or why not?

In this passage Jesus shows us the spirit he expects in those who follow him. Greatness in Jesus' eyes does not come from having many servants but from being the servant of many. *Read John 13:1-17.*

1. According to John, what does Jesus know about himself (vv. 1-3)?

2. In light of that knowledge, what is remarkable about what Jesus does next (vv. 4-5)?

3. Footwashing was normally done by servants or slaves. Why do you think Jesus washes his disciples' feet instead of simply giving them a sermon on love?

4. What tasks at home, at work or in church would be equivalent to footwashing?

5. How do you think Jesus feels as he washes Judas's feet?

How do you think Judas feels?

6. Is Peter simply being humble when he refuses to allow Jesus to serve him (vv. 6-8)? Explain your answer.

7. What spiritual truth is Jesus trying to communicate to Peter (and to us) in verses 8-11?

8. After he finishes washing the disciples' feet, how does Jesus explain the significance of his actions (vv. 12-17)?

9. What does this chapter reveal to you about your attitude toward serving?

10. Among the people you live and work with, what would it mean to "practice footwashing"—to model the humility of Jesus?

Ask God to cultivate a humble spirit in you.

Now or Later

When we think of great people we don't usually include servants on our list. But in Jesus' kingdom the ways of the world are often reversed. The place of honor in Jesus' organizational "pyramid" is not toward the top. Instead the pyramid is turned over on its point. What counts is not how many people are "under" your authority but how many people you serve in love (see Matthew 20:26-27). Envision how your workplace or home would operate differently if that servant mentality was a consistent reality.

15

A Traitor?
Not Me!

We all knew Bill was a snitch. Any comment he could twist into a criticism or complaint, any action he could portray as a breach of company policy was reported to our boss within minutes. Bill couldn't be trusted!

GROUP DISCUSSION. If you knew a close friend was going to falsely betray you, and the betrayal would cost you your job, what would you do?

PERSONAL REFLECTION. Has someone in your life ever hurt you deeply? What was your response to him or her?

If we had been one of Jesus' disciples, we would probably have found it difficult to be around Peter. He was blunt and, at times, arrogant. On the other hand, we might have regarded Judas with trust and respect. The only one who saw deeply enough to discern the true character of these men was Jesus. *Read John 13:18-38.*

1. What tone of voice do you think Jesus uses in verse 21?

in verse 26?

in verse 27?

2. Evidently the disciples did not know who would betray Jesus (v. 22). What does this tell you about how Jesus had treated Judas?

3. How do the disciples interpret Jesus' instruction to Judas in verse 27 (vv. 28-29)?

4. Can we apply Jesus' example to the way we should treat our "betrayers," or was this a unique situation that really doesn't apply today? Explain your answer.

5. What is "new" about Jesus' command in verse 34?

6. John later wrote, "This is how we know what love is: Jesus Christ laid down his life for us. And we ought to lay down our lives for our brothers" (1 John 3:16). In what practical ways can we exhibit this sacrificial love?

7. Why does that kind of love convince all of humanity that we are Jesus' disciples (v. 35)?

_____

8. Do you think Peter's declaration in verse 37 comes from pride or from sincerity? Explain why you came to that conclusion.

_____

9. Three people stand out in this passage—Jesus, Judas and Peter. What one character quality of each—good or evil—makes the greatest impression of you?

_____

10. What can you do to avoid the failures and to follow after the strengths of each main character?

Let God speak to you about any areas of spiritual weakness or vulnerability in your life. Pray for a strong faith that will keep you from turning away from the Lord in a crisis.

Now or Later

On a scale of 1 (low) to 10 (exceptional), how does your church or Christian community rank against the standard of love Jesus spells out in verses 34 and 35? What can you do personally to increase the score?

16

Comfort for a
Troubled Heart

John 14

The call came late at night. A broken sob was followed by these words: "Our son is dying. Will you please come to the hospital?" As I made the trip through darkened streets, I wondered what I could say to bring comfort to these heartbroken parents.

GROUP DISCUSSION. Who is the person you most want to be around when you are hurting? What is it about that person that brings comfort to you?

PERSONAL REFLECTION. Think of a friend who is going through a personal crisis. If you were with that person now, how would you try to help him or her?

Jesus faced the challenge of dealing with broken hearts too. In this chapter he comforts eleven disciples who feel like their world is coming unglued. *Read John 14:1-14.*

1. What does Jesus say in chapter 13 that causes his disciples to have "troubled" hearts (v. 1)?

2. How would the promises Jesus makes in verses 1-4 bring comfort to his disciples?

---

3. After being with Jesus for over three years, what had both Thomas and Philip failed to realize about him (vv. 5-14)?

---

4. Put Jesus' statement in verses 6 and 7 in your own words. In light of those verses, how would you answer someone who thinks there are "many ways to God"?

---

5. *Read John 14:15-31.* Another source of comfort for these troubled disciples would be the Holy Spirit. What does the title Counselor (v. 16) tell us about the Spirit's ministry?

---

6. In what specific ways is the Spirit willing to bring comfort and help in your life (vv. 15-27)?

---

7. What is the relationship between our love and obedience to Jesus and his love and presence in our lives (vv. 15-24)?

How is this different from legalism—trying to earn Jesus' love and presence through our good works?

8. How does the peace Jesus offers differ from the peace offered by the world (vv. 25-31)?

9. How can Jesus' teaching help you counsel a friend who is going through a crisis or who has a troubled heart?

10. Where do you need Jesus' peace in your life right now?

11. What words of Jesus in this passage are most significant to you personally?

Give whatever is troubling you to the Lord and wait in his presence for his comfort and peace.

Now or Later

Think of a friend who is going through a difficult time. Plan to do something this week to encourage that person. A phone call, a letter, a small gift, or an invitation to lunch or a sporting event might be a wonderful blessing in his or her life.

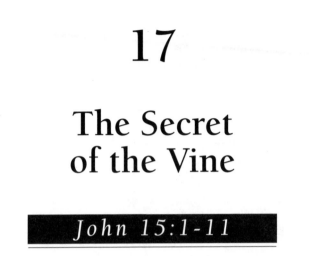

17

The Secret of the Vine

John 15:1-11

The final weekend before Christmas is not the time to visit a shopping mall. If you are fortunate enough to find a parking spot, the press of people inside makes shopping almost impossible. On one expedition I heard a mother giving final instructions to her young son before plunging into the crowd: "Stay close to me and hold my hand all the time. We won't get separated if we hold on to each other."

GROUP DISCUSSION. When you were a child, did you try to stay close to your parents in an unfamiliar place, or did you tend to wander away? Describe a memory (or fear) of being lost.

PERSONAL REFLECTION. Have you ever felt far from Christ since becoming a Christian? What circumstances made you feel that way?

As Jesus prepared his disciples to face life without his visible presence, he impressed on them the importance of staying close to him spiritually. He said, "Remain in me." If you've ever longed to understand the secret of spiritual growth, you will find it in Jesus' words to us in John 15. *Read John 15:1-11.*

1. Jesus' instruction to his disciples in this passage revolves around three symbols—the vine, the gardener and the branches. What is Jesus trying to communicate by calling himself the "true vine"?

2. What is the significance of calling his disciples "branches"?

3. Instead of commanding us to bear fruit, why is Jesus' only command "Remain in me" (v. 4)?

4. What does it mean to remain in Christ?

5. The fruit produced by the remaining branch is sometimes viewed as a reference to new converts. But branches produce grapes, not other branches. What other possible meanings are there for *fruit?*

6. The Father's ministry as the gardener is to "[cut] off every branch . . . that bears no fruit" (v. 2). What do you think that means?

7. The Father prunes fruitful branches to make them *more* fruitful (v. 2). In what ways have you experienced the Father's "pruning," and what were the results?

8. What spiritual benefits result from remaining in Christ (vv. 7-11)?

---

9. There are three categories of branches described in this passage—those bearing no fruit, those bearing some fruit and those bearing much fruit. In which category would you place yourself, and why?

---

10. If you are not bearing much fruit, what is Jesus' counsel to you in these verses?

Picture yourself as a vine bearing abundant, healthy fruit. Ask God to help you become the person he desires you to be.

Now or Later

What hesitancy do you have about cultivating your relationship with Jesus?

What are some specific things you can do to deepen your relationship with Jesus?

18

The Cost
of Friendship

John 15:12—16:4

During his life on earth, Jesus did not surround himself with a group
of students or even a group of followers. He placed himself in the
company of friends. I used to think it was a sign of spiritual strength
when someone said, "I don't really need other people. I just need the
Lord." Now I see it as a sign of immaturity. Close relationships are
Christlike!

GROUP DISCUSSION. What are some of the most important qualities in
a friend?

PERSONAL REFLECTION. Who is your closest friend? Take some time to
pray for that person as you begin this study.

As Jesus continues his conversation with his disciples, Jesus shows us
what friendship with him is really like. There is both comfort and
cost. *Read John 15:12-17.*

---

1. Jesus already told his disciples to love each other (John 13:34-35).
How does his instruction in verse 12 raise the standard of our love?

2. What are the requirements and benefits of friendship with Jesus (vv. 14-17)?

3. Is being a friend of Jesus the same as being a believer in Jesus? Explain.

4. *Read John 15:18-25.* Why does Jesus switch from talking about love to talk about hate?

5. What reasons does Jesus give for the world's hatred?

6. Give one or two specific examples of how you have experienced the world's hatred as a Christian. How did you respond to the hostility at the time?

7. What does Jesus mean when he says that without his coming, his words and his miracles, the world "would not be guilty of sin" (vv. 22-25)?

8. *Read John 15:26—16:4.* In what ways will the Counselor and the disciples themselves continue the ministry begun by Jesus (vv. 26-27)?

9. What kind of treatment can the disciples expect from those who do not know Christ (16:1-4)?

10. What kinds of persecution are most probable for us in our society? Explain your answer.

11. If we as Christians are not persecuted in some way, what might that imply about our spiritual commitment?

Pray for strength to face opposition with the same courage and grace that Jesus demonstrated.

Now or Later

Most Christians in democratic societies face very little serious persecution for their faith. Christians in other parts of the world, however, often have to endure imprisonment, poverty, slavery and even death for their commitment to Christ. Check out some websites of organizations that help persecuted Christians. Read some of their literature. Pray for your brothers and sisters in distress.

19

Secrets of the Spirit

John 16:5-15

A lovely woman in our church died not long ago. She knew for almost a year that unless the Lord intervened, the cancer in her brain would kill her. That year gave her time and opportunity to express her love for her husband and family and to say goodbye. She used the hours left of her life to pass on godly wisdom and encouragement to every life she touched.

GROUP DISCUSSION. How are you at saying goodbye?

Is it easier for you to be the person leaving or the person left behind? Why?

PERSONAL REFLECTION. What would you want to tell your family or closest friends if you knew that you had only a short time to live?

In John 16 Jesus knows that he will die in less than twenty-four hours. When his disciples are faced with that reality, they become troubled (14:1), then afraid (14:27) and finally filled with grief (16:6). Jesus responds to each of their concerns by talking about the coming Holy Spirit. *Read John 16:5-15.*

1. Based on what Jesus says in these verses, how would you describe the mood among the disciples?

How would you have felt if you had been there?

2. Jesus says that it is for the disciples' good that he should leave and that the Counselor should come. Why is the Spirit's presence more profitable to the disciples than Jesus' presence?

3. In what ways is it more profitable today to have the Holy Spirit actively present than to have Jesus here on earth?

4. What does Jesus say the Spirit's ministry would be toward the world (vv. 8-11)?

5. How does the Spirit do the same work today in the hearts of people who have not believed in Jesus?

6. "The prince of this world" mentioned in verse 11 is Satan, our spiritual enemy. In what way does Satan "now stand condemned"?

7. Why is it important for the Holy Spirit to convince the world that its "prince" is already condemned?

8. What can we infer from verses 8-11 about our part in bringing people to faith in Christ?

What is the Spirit's responsibility in bringing people to faith in Christ?

9. One of the Spirit's ministries is communication. What specific things did Jesus say the Spirit would communicate to the disciples (vv. 12-15)?

10. How does the Spirit guide us into God's truth and bring glory to Jesus today?

11. What spiritual truth would you like to ask the Holy Spirit to help you understand?

Ask God the Holy Spirit to teach you and to exalt Jesus in your life.

Now or Later
One of the roles of the Holy Spirit is to bring glory (as in attention, honor) to Jesus (John 16:14). Do you think your church or Christian fellowship puts too much emphasis on the Holy Spirit, too little emphasis or just about the right emphasis? How can you "test" the Spirit's presence in a worship or praise service?

20

Peace in a Time of Trouble

John 16:16-33

Those who follow Jesus are not shielded from life's deepest problems. We must still face sorrow, rejection and heartache. We see our loved ones die, we see relationships fail, and sometimes our children go their own way rather than God's way. What makes a Christian different is not the absence of difficulty but the presence of a Comforter. We never walk life's valleys alone.

GROUP DISCUSSION. Trace the story of a painful experience in your life. How did God help you during that time of struggle?

PERSONAL REFLECTION. Who do you turn to first when you are in sorrow or pain? How does that person comfort you?

Jesus gives us some very practical help in these verses for facing life's crises. He doesn't answer all our questions, but he gives us what we need to survive. *Read John 16:16-24.*

1. It is obvious that the disciples are confused and concerned about Jesus' statements (vv. 16-18). Why do you think they are so upset?

2. Jesus answers their questions not by giving them an explanation but by making them a promise (vv. 19-22). What is the promise?

Why would it bring them joy in the middle of their grief and confusion?

---

3. How can this incident help us when our questions to the Lord seemingly go unanswered?

---

4. What new promise regarding prayer does Jesus give his disciples (vv. 23-24)?

---

5. How would that promise make their joy complete?

---

6. What connection can you make for your own life between problems, prayer and joy?

7. *Read John 16:25-33.* How would Jesus' assurance of the Father's love help the disciples in the days just ahead of them?

---

8. In verse 32 Jesus predicts that his disciples will abandon him. How will Jesus' promise of peace and victory (v. 33) sustain and help you after a time of failure?

---

9. Which of the promises in this chapter has made the deepest impression on you, and why?

---

10. How can you use these promises to strengthen a friend who is going through trials or discouragement?

Give God whatever grief or sorrow you are carrying. Open yourself to the Spirit's peace.

Now or Later

Both Jesus and the world offer a form of joy (John 15:11; 16:22-24), peace (John 14:27; 16:33) and love (John 13:34-35; 15:9-19). What is the difference between what the world offers and what Jesus offers? How have you experienced both types of love, joy and peace?

21

Jesus Prays for Us

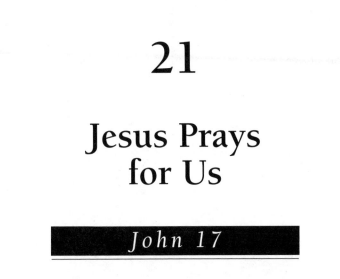

John 17

I work as a chaplain for a hospice organization, and I talk with a lot of people who know they are near death. Sometimes we chat about their memories of life; more often we discuss the realities of the next life. The one thing I have noticed is that the approach of death has a way of bringing our priorities into very sharp focus. People who know death is imminent also know what is really important in life and who they really care about.

GROUP DISCUSSION. Other than your relationship with the Lord, what two or three relationships are most valuable to you? What one thing would you ask God to do for each of those important people?

PERSONAL REFLECTION. What goal do you want to reach before the end of your life? What are you doing today to help you reach that goal?

In Jesus' final prayer with his disciples, he prays for himself, for them and for you! Every believer is on Jesus' mind as he faces the greatest trial of his life—the cross. *Read John 17.*

1. Jesus makes only one request for himself—that the Father would glorify him so he might glorify the Father. Why do you think that was so important to Jesus?

———————————————————————————————

2. To what extent is God's glory foremost in your mind on a daily basis? Explain your answer.

———————————————————————————————

3. How is Jesus' definition of eternal life (v. 3) different from merely living forever?

———————————————————————————————

4. According to verses 6-19, what specific ministries does Jesus have toward his disciples?

———————————————————————————————

5. Twice Jesus asks the Father to protect his disciples from the evil one (vv. 11, 15). Why would that protection be so important in Jesus' mind as he faces the cross?

———————————————————————————————

6. Jesus also asks the Father to sanctify his disciples through his Word (v. 17). How can we allow God's Word to have that kind of effect on our lives?

———————————————————————————————

7. Jesus prays that those who believe in him would be one, "so that the world may believe that you have sent me" (vv. 21, 23). Why is our unity a powerful argument for the truth of Jesus' claims?

8. In what practical ways can we demonstrate our oneness with other believers?

9. Jesus obviously prays this prayer out loud to bring comfort and assurance to his disciples. How do Jesus' words encourage or assure you?

10. Jesus does not simply pray for the immediate, urgent needs of himself and his disciples. Instead he focuses on the long-range, important goals of their ministries. How are your prayers like or unlike Jesus' prayer?

Express to God your sincere desire to glorify him in all you do.

Now or Later

Construct your own prayer based on Jesus' model. Pray for yourself, the people closest to you and the people whom you influence in the workplace or neighborhood. What do you want God to accomplish long-range in each person? Now pray the prayer regularly. Refine it as God gives you direction. Watch God work!

22

Trial & Trust

John 18:1-27

Most of us can't imagine being arrested, imprisoned and brought to trial. If we were guilty of a crime, it would be humiliating. But if we were innocent, it would be devastating.

GROUP DISCUSSION. How would you respond if someone falsely accused you of a crime and even called the police to have you arrested?

PERSONAL REFLECTION. What would you do if someone betrayed your best friend?

In what should have been the most demeaning experience of his life, Jesus exhibits majesty and glory. Against a backdrop of attack, betrayal and abandonment, we see the brilliance of Christ's confident trust in the Father. His calm assurance will help us face life's hurts and injustices with the same trust in the same Father. *Read John 18:1-27.*

1. If you had been one of Jesus' disciples, what emotions would have gripped you when the soldiers arrived at the garden?

2. Why would Jesus go to a place where Judas knew he might be found (vv. 1-3)?

3. When the soldiers say they are seeking Jesus of Nazareth, Jesus replies "I am he" (v. 5). How would you explain the reaction of the soldiers (v. 6)?

4. What insight do Peter's action and Jesus' rebuke (v. 11) give you about your attempts to act out of your own strength and wisdom?

5. Think back to the deepest sin of your life. How does a look at your own sin change your attitude toward Peter's denial of Jesus?

6. If you had been in Peter's place, what reasons might you have given for denying that you were a disciple of Jesus?

7. When and where is it hardest for you to openly identify yourself as a Christian?

8. What can we learn from Peter's failure about being prepared to stand against the world's challenges?

9. John writes this account to highlight Jesus' courage, his power and his obedience to the Father. Which aspect of Jesus' character impresses you most?

10. What can you do to more clearly express your loyalty to Jesus when you are around other people?

Admit any fear of identifying with Christ. Ask God to strengthen your faith to answer the world's challenges.

Now or Later

Learn more about what Christian ministries are available to prisoners and their families in your community. Call the chaplain at your county jail or at a nearby state prison. Volunteer to help with a prison service. Pray for the moving of God's Spirit in the hearts of prisoners.

23

Character Test

"Christ killers!" The words made my stomach tighten. Someone had spray-painted the phrase and a series of swastikas on the Jewish synagogue in our city. Anti-Semitism had raised its ugly head again.

The New Testament writers certainly blame the Jewish leaders for condemning Jesus to die. But they didn't act alone. The Roman governor, Pontius Pilate, agreed to the death penalty. He did so even though he knew Jesus was innocent.

GROUP DISCUSSION. To what extent are you tempted to compromise your Christian faith or witness because of pressure from people around you? Describe a situation in which you sensed that pressure.

PERSONAL REFLECTION. Are you a person who stands for what is right, regardless of the consequences, or do you tend to compromise to keep the peace? When have you wished you were more the other way?

In the broader perspective of the plan of God, many people share the blame for Jesus' death. In a sense, all of us killed Jesus—he died for *our* sins and in *our* place. The most amazing answer to the question of who killed Jesus is that no one did! Jesus said, "No one takes my life from me. I lay it down of my own choice." *Read John 18:28-37.*

1. A Roman trial included four basic elements. What events or statements from John's account fall under each category?

The accusation:

The interrogation or search for evidence:

The defense:

The verdict:

---

2. How do the Jewish leaders reveal their hypocrisy by refusing to enter Pilate's (a non-Jewish) home (v. 28)?

---

3. How would you describe Jesus' "kingdom" based on his response to Pilate (vv. 36-37)?

---

4. *Read John 18:38—19:16.* Pilate obviously is trying to release Jesus. What specific attempts does he make?

---

5. How does it make you feel when you read the record of injustice done toward Jesus?

6. What can you conclude about Pilate's character after reading this passage?

———————————————————————————————

7. The Jews' true charge against Jesus comes out in verse 7: "He claimed to be the Son of God." Why do you think Pilate reacts to that statement the way he does (19:8-9)?

———————————————————————————————

8. Why doesn't Jesus say more to Pilate and defend himself more vigorously (19:9-11)?

———————————————————————————————

9. What would you have done if you had been Pilate?

———————————————————————————————

10. What does this passage teach you about how to respond when you are treated unjustly?

Ask Jesus, who faced Pilate's injustice with courage and grace, to give you the strength to stand firmly for what is right and good.

Now or Later

In the middle of a degrading experience, Jesus is portrayed as a King. Who or what are some of the "kings" people obey today?

Who or what competes with Christ for authority over your life?

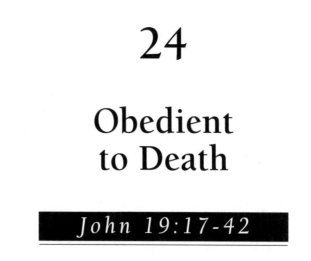

24

Obedient
to Death

John 19:17-42

There is nothing pleasant or attractive about an execution. The only one I've ever seen was in a televised news report from Vietnam. A captured soldier was shot. It left a knot in my stomach for days.

GROUP DISCUSSION. Tell about how a national or international assassination affected you and how you learned about the tragedy.

PERSONAL REFLECTION. When you think about death, what feelings and thoughts come to mind?

In Jesus' day execution was designed to be public and painful. The account of the crucifixion is not easy to read. You may be tempted to think that Jesus' death was a cruel mistake. It wasn't. Jesus' life was not taken from him; he laid it down willingly. His cross was, in a very real sense, our cross. *Read John 19:17-42.*

1. Crucifixion was obviously a brutal and tortuous form of execution. Why do you think John leaves so much of the agonizing detail out of his account?

2. Three groups are involved in Jesus' death—the soldiers, the Jewish leaders and Pilate. How would you characterize each one's attitude toward Jesus?

3. In what ways do their attitudes toward Jesus parallel those of men and women today?

4. How do you think Mary, Jesus' mother, feels as she stands by the cross?

5. How is Jesus' tender care for her evident even while he is dying (vv. 26-27)?

6. What is the significance of Jesus' cry, "It is finished" (v. 30; see John 17:4)?

7. What feelings and thoughts would have gone through your mind if you had helped prepare Jesus' body for burial?

8. Where are Jesus' disciples during his crucifixion and burial (see John 16:32)?

Why do you think they are so conspicuously absent?

---

9. Under the same circumstances, do you think you would have been more like Joseph and Nicodemus or Jesus' disciples? Explain your answer.

---

10. When it comes to public identification with Jesus, how is it possible to respond in the same ways today?

---

11. What aspect of Jesus' death has made the deepest impression on you and why?

Thank Jesus for enduring the cross so that you could be forgiven and restored to a right relationship with God.

Now or Later

Some critics of the Bible claim that Jesus never really died on the cross. What evidence does John provide that refutes that view? Why was it so important for John to establish the certainty of Jesus' death?

25

The Son Is Up!

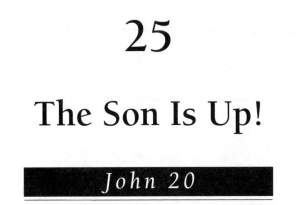

John 20

The story circulated for days in the hospital where my brother worked. An orderly was told to take a body to the morgue. Simply out of habit, the orderly felt the man's wrist for a pulse. When he realized his mistake, the orderly quickly dropped the arm, but not before his sensitive fingers told him something his mind struggled to believe. There was a pulse! The doctors were called, and the man was revived.

GROUP DISCUSSION. How would you react if a friend told you he had seen someone raised from the dead?

PERSONAL REFLECTION. Why is it important to you that Jesus rose from the dead? Could you still believe in him if he had died and we could visit his tomb?

The hospital story my brother told me may or may not be fully accurate. But I know of one account of a man coming back to life that is true. The man lived for years after the event. In fact, he is still alive! *Read John 20.*

---

1. John identifies three witnesses to the empty tomb: Mary Magdalene, Peter and "the other disciple" (John himself). What important details do we learn from each one (vv. 1-9)?

2. Why is it important to prove the tomb was empty?

3. John also records three appearances of the risen Christ: to Mary Magdalene, to his disciples and to Thomas. Why do you think Mary Magdalene doesn't immediately recognize Jesus (vv. 10-15)?

After she does recognize him, what impresses you most about their encounter (vv. 16-18)?

4. When Jesus appears to his disciples, what specific gifts and promises does he give them (vv. 19-23)?

What do you think is the significance of each gift or promise?

5. Finally, Jesus appears to Thomas (vv. 24-29). How does Thomas's attitude—both before and after Jesus appears to him—add credibility to the resurrection?

6. How does Thomas's exclamation "My Lord and my God" (v. 28) provide a fitting climax to John's Gospel?

_____

7. What can we learn from Jesus' encounter with Thomas about helping people who have doubts about the Christian message?

_____

8. On what evidence do you base your belief that Jesus rose from the dead?

_____

9. Is believing that Jesus rose from the dead as important as believing that he died on the cross for our sins? Explain why or why not.

_____

10. John tells us why he has written his Gospel in verses 30 and 31. Of all the "miraculous signs" John has included, which have been most convincing to you, and why?

Praise Jesus as your risen Savior. Use Thomas's words, "My Lord and my God," as you address Jesus.

Now or Later

Mary Magdalene wanted to hold on to Jesus, but Jesus sent her on a mission to tell others that he was alive. Who is someone you can tell about Jesus and his resurrection? Make a plan to talk with that person this week. Ask God to give you an opportunity to share the message.

26

A Walk with a Resurrected Man

John 21

Most of us find it easier to forgive than to forget. We may be ready to forgive someone who has hurt us deeply, but we have a hard time trusting that person again.

GROUP DISCUSSION. Tell the group about a broken relationship you tried to restore and what resulted from your effort.

PERSONAL REFLECTION. Describe how you feel when someone you have hurt refuses to forgive you.

Peter failed Jesus miserably. He promised to give up his life if necessary to protect Jesus but then denied even knowing him a few hours later. Peter knew Jesus had forgiven him. The question that pressed on Peter's heart was, Would Jesus trust him again? Could Jesus still use him to bring glory to God? *Read John 21:1-14.*

1. What is the significance of Peter's decision to return to fishing (vv. 1-3)?

2. What is Jesus trying to show the disciples by allowing them to catch such a large number of fish (vv. 4-6; see Luke 5:4-11)?

3. When Peter hears that "it is the Lord" (vv. 7-8), he jumps into the water and begins swimming ahead of the boat. What does that response reveal about Peter and his relationship with Jesus?

4. How would you have responded if you had denied Jesus just a few days earlier?

5. *Read John 21:15-25.* What subtle differences do you notice in Jesus' three questions and Peter's responses (vv. 15-17)?

What do you think is the significance of those differences?

6. What can we learn from this passage about the steps involved in restoring a Christian who has sinned?

7. Why do you think Jesus chooses this particular occasion to predict the kind of death Peter would die (vv. 18-19)?

8. How does it help to know that you can still serve and glorify God no matter what your past failures have been?

9. What does Jesus' rebuke to Peter (v. 22) reveal about the danger of comparing ourselves with other Christians?

10. Picture Jesus saying these things to you. How would you respond, or what would the words mean in the context of your life?

"Do you truly love me?"

"Take care of my sheep."

"You must follow me."

Express your willingness to do whatever Jesus asks you to do.

Now or Later
As you have studied John's Gospel, what aspects of Jesus' character or ministry have impressed you most?

What responses have you made in your heart and life as a result of that deeper understanding?

Leader's Notes

Leading a Bible discussion can be an enjoyable and rewarding experience. But it can also be *scary*—especially if you've never done it before. If this is your feeling, you're in good company. When God asked Moses to lead the Israelites out of Egypt, he replied, "O Lord, please send someone else to do it"! (Ex 4:13). It was the same with Solomon, Jeremiah and Timothy, but God helped these people in spite of their weaknesses, and he will help you as well.

You don't need to be an expert on the Bible or a trained teacher to lead a Bible discussion. The idea behind these inductive studies is that the leader guides group members to discover for themselves what the Bible has to say. This method of learning will allow group members to remember much more of what is said than a lecture would.

These studies are designed to be led easily. As a matter of fact, the flow of questions through the passage from observation to interpretation to application is so natural that you may feel that the studies lead themselves. This study guide is also flexible. You can use it with a variety of groups—student, professional, neighborhood or church groups. Each study takes forty-five to sixty minutes in a group setting.

There are some important facts to know about group dynamics and encouraging discussion. The suggestions listed below should enable you to effectively and enjoyably fulfill your role as leader.

Preparing for the Study

1. Ask God to help you understand and apply the passage in your own life. Unless this happens, you will not be prepared to lead others. Pray too for the various members of the group. Ask God to open your hearts to the message of his Word and motivate you to action.

2. Read the introduction to the entire guide to get an overview of the

entire book and the issues which will be explored.

3. As you begin each study, read and reread the assigned Bible passage to familiarize yourself with it.

4. This study guide is based on the New International Version of the Bible. It will help you and the group if you use this translation as the basis for your study and discussion.

5. Carefully work through each question in the study. Spend time in meditation and reflection as you consider how to respond.

6. Write your thoughts and responses in the space provided in the study guide. This will help you to express your understanding of the passage clearly.

7. It might help to have a Bible dictionary handy. Use it to look up any unfamiliar words, names or places. (For additional help on how to study a passage, see chapter five of *How to Lead a LifeGuide Bible Study,* InterVarsity Press.)

8. Consider how you can apply the Scripture to your life. Remember that the group will follow your lead in responding to the studies. They will not go any deeper than you do.

9. Once you have finished your own study of the passage, familiarize yourself with the leader's notes for the study you are leading. These are designed to help you in several ways. First, they tell you the purpose the study guide author had in mind when writing the study. Take time to think through how the study questions work together to accomplish that purpose. Second, the notes provide you with additional background information or suggestions on group dynamics for various questions. This information can be useful when people have difficulty understanding or answering a question. Third, the leader's notes can alert you to potential problems you may encounter during the study.

10. If you wish to remind yourself of anything mentioned in the leader's notes, make a note to yourself below that question in the study.

Leading the Study

1. Begin the study on time. Open with prayer, asking God to help the group to understand and apply the passage.

2. Be sure that everyone in your group has a study guide. Encourage the group to prepare beforehand for each discussion by reading the introduction to the guide and by working through the questions in the study.

3. At the beginning of your first time together, explain that these studies are meant to be discussions, not lectures. Encourage the members of the group to participate. However, do not put pressure on those who may be hes-

itant to speak during the first few sessions. You may want to suggest the following guidelines to your group.

☐ Stick to the topic being discussed.

☐ Your responses should be based on the verses which are the focus of the discussion and not on outside authorities such as commentaries or speakers.

☐ These studies focus on a particular passage of Scripture. Only rarely should you refer to other portions of the Bible. This allows for everyone to participate in in-depth study on equal ground.

☐ Anything said in the group is considered confidential and will not be discussed outside the group unless specific permission is given to do so.

☐ We will listen attentively to each other and provide time for each person present to talk.

☐ We will pray for each other.

4. Have a group member read the introduction at the beginning of the discussion.

5. Every session begins with a group discussion question. The question or activity is meant to be used before the passage is read. The question introduces the theme of the study and encourages group members to begin to open up. Encourage as many members as possible to participate, and be ready to get the discussion going with your own response.

This section is designed to reveal where our thoughts or feelings need to be transformed by Scripture. That is why it is especially important not to read the passage before the discussion question is asked. The passage will tend to color the honest reactions people would otherwise give because they are, of course, supposed to think the way the Bible does.

You may want to supplement the group discussion question with an icebreaker to help people to get comfortable. See the community section of *Small Group Idea Book* for more ideas.

You also might want to use the personal reflection question with your group. Either allow a time of silence for people to respond individually or discuss it together.

6. Have a group member (or members if the passage is long) read aloud the passage to be studied. Then give people several minutes to read the passage again silently so that they can take it all in.

7. Question 1 will generally be an overview question designed to briefly survey the passage. Encourage the group to look at the whole passage, but try to avoid getting sidetracked by questions or issues that will be addressed later in the study.

8. As you ask the questions, keep in mind that they are designed to be used just as they are written. You may simply read them aloud. Or you may prefer to express them in your own words.

There may be times when it is appropriate to deviate from the study guide. For example, a question may have already been answered. If so, move on to the next question. Or someone may raise an important question not covered in the guide. Take time to discuss it, but try to keep the group from going off on tangents.

9. Avoid answering your own questions. If necessary, repeat or rephrase them until they are clearly understood. Or point out something you read in the leader's notes to clarify the context or meaning. An eager group quickly becomes passive and silent if they think the leader will do most of the talking.

10. Don't be afraid of silence. People may need time to think about the question before formulating their answers.

11. Don't be content with just one answer. Ask, "What do the rest of you think?" or "Anything else?" until several people have given answers to the question.

12. Acknowledge all contributions. Try to be affirming whenever possible. Never reject an answer. If it is clearly off-base, ask, "Which verse led you to that conclusion?" or again, "What do the rest of you think?"

13. Don't expect every answer to be addressed to you, even though this will probably happen at first. As group members become more at ease, they will begin to truly interact with each other. This is one sign of healthy discussion.

14. Don't be afraid of controversy. It can be very stimulating. If you don't resolve an issue completely, don't be frustrated. Move on and keep it in mind for later. A subsequent study may solve the problem.

15. Periodically summarize what the group has said about the passage. This helps to draw together the various ideas mentioned and gives continuity to the study. But don't preach.

16. At the end of the Bible discussion you may want to allow group members a time of quiet to work on an idea under "Now or Later." Then discuss what you experienced. Or you may want to encourage group members to work on these ideas between meetings. Give an opportunity during the session for people to talk about what they are learning.

17. Conclude your time together with conversational prayer, adapting the prayer suggestion at the end of the study to your group. Ask for God's help in following through on the commitments you've made.

18. End on time.

Many more suggestions and helps are found in *How to Lead a LifeGuide Bible Study*, which is part of the LifeGuide Bible Study series.

Components of Small Groups
A healthy small group should do more than study the Bible. There are four components to consider as you structure your time together.

Nurture. Small groups help us to grow in our knowledge and love of God. Bible study is the key to making this happen and is the foundation of your small group.

Community. Small groups are a great place to develop deep friendships with other Christians. Allow time for informal interaction before and after each study. Plan activities and games that will help you get to know each other. Spend time having fun together—going on a picnic or cooking dinner together.

Worship and prayer. Your study will be enhanced by spending time praising God together in prayer or song. Pray for each other's needs—and keep track of how God is answering prayer in your group. Ask God to help you to apply what you are learning in your study.

Outreach. Reaching out to others can be a practical way of applying what you are learning, and it will keep your group from becoming self-focused. Host a series of evangelistic discussions for your friends or neighbors. Clean up the yard of an elderly friend. Serve at a soup kitchen together, or spend a day working on a Habitat house.

Many more suggestions and helps in each of these areas are found in *Small Group Idea Book*. Information on building a small group can be found in *Small Group Leaders' Handbook* and *The Big Book on Small Groups* (both from InterVarsity Press). Reading through one of these books would be worth your time.

PART 1. JESUS, THE LIVING WORD OF GOD.

Almost every statement I have made about the Gospel of John in the introduction to the study guide has been challenged by some New Testament scholar! I have written from the position held by most evangelical students of John's Gospel. As group leader it might be helpful for you to read a conservative introduction to the Gospel. The standard work (both introduction and commentary) is by Leon Morris (*The Gospel According to John*, New International Commentaries on the New Testament [Grand Rapids, Mich.: Eerdmans, 1971]). It is a scholarly study but filled with insight and devotion to Christ.

Other good sources are

Bruce Milne, *The Message of John,* The Bible Speaks Today (Downers Grove, Ill.: InterVarsity Press, 1993).

Gary Burge, *John,* NIV Application Commentary (Grand Rapids, Mich.: Zondervan, 1999).

One profitable way to introduce your group to John's Gospel is to compare the four Gospels in regard to their authorship, audience, purpose and message. In that way you can emphasize John's unique contribution to our understanding of Jesus Christ. Any Bible handbook will give you help in putting together such a comparison. More information is available on the page for this study guide at the IVP website <www.ivpress.com>.

Study 1. John 1. Encountering the Word.

Purpose: To introduce John's message about Jesus and to demonstrate the impact Jesus had in people's lives.

General note. The first eighteen verses of John's Gospel (often called the prologue) are not as much an introduction to the Gospel as they are a condensation of John's whole message. John states the basic truths about Jesus that he wants to communicate to us and then uses the remainder of the book to prove what he says in the prologue.

Group discussion. To have a little fun with this question, you might have each person write their answer on a slip of paper and put it in a hat. Draw the answers out and see if you can guess whose is whose.

Question 1. By calling Jesus "the Word" John was declaring that Jesus is the full expression of God to us. Just as we express our thoughts to others through words, God expressed himself to humanity in Jesus. Jesus came to show us who God is. A good parallel passage is Hebrews 1:1-2.

Question 2. The assertion in John 1:1 that "the Word was God" is challenged by some modern cults. Jehovah's Witnesses contend, for example, that because no definite article appears before the word *God* in the Greek text, this phrase should be translated "the Word was a god." No competent Greek scholar agrees with that translation. The absence of the definite article stresses that Jesus was distinct from the Father but was fully God just the same. For further details, see Morris, *Gospel According to John,* pp. 76-78.

Question 3. John uses a form of the word *believe* ninety-eight times in his Gospel. His primary purpose was to bring his readers to actively believe in Jesus, to place their trust in him and in his promises. John divides all humanity into two groups—those who believe in Jesus and those who do not believe, those who have eternal life and those who do not. Faith is not a static, one-time event for John but a dynamic, growing, active process.

Question 6. John the Baptist repeatedly declared that he was not the Christ (the promised Messiah) nor a reincarnated Old Testament prophet. He was a voice, a witness to the light. John resisted any labels of greatness for himself. John also made it clear that the Messiah was superior to him in character, in ministry and in authority. When John saw the Holy Spirit descend on his relative Jesus, John knew that Jesus was the one he had been waiting for (Jn 1:32-34).

Question 8. These five men eventually became part of Jesus' permanent band of disciples. All of them had been influenced by John the Baptist's message, so they were looking for the Messiah. Even when they found him, however, some expressed doubt and skepticism.

Study 2. John 2. Signs of God.

Purpose: To confront us with Jesus' power over creation and his authority as God's anointed Deliver.

Question 2. In Jesus' day the wedding feast for the family and friends of the bride and groom lasted between two and seven days. The groom's parents were responsible for feeding and caring for all the guests the entire time. If they ran out of food or wine during the feast, it was considered a serious insult to the guests.

The Gospels never refer to Joseph as alive during Jesus' adult years. Probably Joseph died when Jesus was a young adult. As the oldest son, Jesus had the responsibility of caring for Mary and helping her. It was natural, then, in this time of need for Mary to come to Jesus for assistance.

Question 4. Jesus' miracle was a suspension and compression of natural law. Saint Augustine pointed out: "He who made the wine at this wedding does the same thing every year in the vines. As the water which the servants put into the water pots was turned into wine by the Lord, so that which the clouds pour down is turned into wine by the same Lord." It is also significant that Jesus isn't content with producing mediocre wine. He creates wine of superior quality.

This miracle is the first of seven "signs" that John uses to portray Jesus as God the Son. The others are the healing of the nobleman's son (Jn 4:46-53); the healing of the lame man (Jn 5:5-16); the provision of food for five thousand people (Jn 6:1-15); walking on water (Jn 6:16-21); the healing of the blind man (Jn 9:1-38); and the raising of Lazarus from the dead (Jn 11:1-44).

Question 6. The scene shifts in these verses from Cana to Jerusalem. Jesus went to Jerusalem to be with his family and his disciples for the celebration of Passover.

Passover was a great feast day commemorating Israel's deliverance from Egypt. Instead of leading the people into a time of worship and praise to God, however, the temple leaders used it as an opportunity to make money. Those selling animals were agents of the high priest, who sold "approved" sacrificial animals usually at three to five times their market value.

The priestly leaders had also determined that the annual temple tax could be paid only in Judean coinage. Jews from other parts of the Roman Empire who came to Jerusalem to worship had to exchange their foreign coins for Judean coins at a very high profit for the money exchangers. The entire system was run as a monopoly by Annas, the high priest. In the popular language of the day, the temple courtyard was called "the Bazaar of Annas."

Jesus' actions in the temple meant lost profits for the priestly leaders. They now had a reason to hate Jesus. This was the first of two cleansings that Jesus carried out. This one came early in his ministry; the second came just a few days before his crucifixion (Mk 11:15-18; Mt 21:12-17).

Question 8. The disciples recognized Jesus' action as a fulfillment of Old Testament prophecy (v. 17; see Ps 69:9).

Question 10. Jesus knew that the allegiance of the crowd was weak and subject to change. He refused to get caught in the trap of trying to please people. His concern was to please his Father.

Study 3. John 3. Starting Over.

Purpose: To grasp the meaning and life-changing significance of new birth.

Question 2. Birth is just one of many New Testament pictures of what results when a person believes in Jesus Christ, but it is a powerful tool for helping people understand the complete transformation Jesus brings.

Question 3. Nicodemus (nick-o-dee-mus) was amazed at Jesus' insistence on a new birth because he put a great deal of trust in his first birth as a Jew. The Scriptures, however, revealed that more was needed for salvation than physical birth into the people of Israel. Men and women needed a new heart—a transformation before God (Jer 31:33; see also Rom 3:28-29).

As Jesus talked, Nicodemus began to recognize the importance of spiritual birth. His question in verse 4, however, centered on how it could happen. Jesus responded by showing Nicodemus that the means of this new birth are not physical but spiritual. In order to receive this new birth, a person must be born not only of "water" or "flesh"—that is, born physically—but also of the Spirit. Only the Spirit of God can bring life to the human spirit. (The question of what Jesus meant by the phrase "born of water" has been widely debated by commentators and theologians. I have interpreted *water* to be parallel to *flesh*, which refers to natural birth.)

Question 4. Jesus calls Nicodemus "Israel's teacher," a reference to Nicodemus's reputation as an authority on the Scriptures. Jesus is amazed that Nicodemus doesn't understand the heart of a genuine relationship with God. Men and women in the Old Testament age were not made right with God by keeping the regulations of the law. They were made right with God by grace through faith. They were called to believe in the Lord God. Obedience to the law was the *result* of true faith, not the way of salvation.

Question 5. The people of Israel only had to look at the brass serpent in faith in order to be delivered from death. We have only to look to Jesus in faith to be delivered from sin's eternal "bite" of death.

Question 6. Salvation emerges from God's desire to redeem those he created. God took the initiative in love to provide for us what we could not provide for ourselves. God came in grace to pay the penalty that his holy justice demanded.

Question 8. You may want to call on one or two committed Christians in the group to share their answer to this question rather than to single out the suspected or known non-Christians. At some point during your study of John, try to talk privately with those who are unclear about the gospel or their own commitment to Christ.

Question 11. This is a good place to emphasize the importance of following Christ in obedience (John the Baptist) as the direct result of being born again (Nicodemus). Both aspects of the Christian walk are discussed in chapter 3: the new birth and a new life under the lordship of Christ.

Study 4. John 4. Connecting with People.

Purpose: To equip us to minister effectively to people whom God brings into our lives every day.

Question 1. Jewish hatred of Samaritans had deep historical and religious roots. Seven hundred and fifty years before Jesus' day, the Assyrians invaded the northern section of Israel and deported the people living there. They left only a few poor Jews in the land. Then the Assyrians imported other conquered people and settled them in the former Jewish territory. The pagan, non-Jewish population intermarried with the Jewish people and produced a mixed racial group called the Samaritans. The orthodox Jews in southern Palestine looked at the Samaritans as a corrupt people and took great pains to remain separate from them. It was the accepted custom that Jews and Samaritans would not drink from the same vessel.

Question 2. By asking for water, Jesus was deliberately crossing three cultural barriers. The first barrier was sexual: he talked to a woman. Jewish men were advised never to talk to any women in public. The second barrier was racial: the woman was a Samaritan; Jesus was a Jew. The third barrier was moral: the woman was living in an immoral relationship with a man to whom she was not married (v. 18); Jesus was the Son of God. Jesus was willing to cross those barriers in order to reach a woman who needed to believe in him.

Question 3. *Living water* normally referred to running water, such as would be found in a river or stream. It was greatly preferred over still water, especially for ritual purification. Jesus drew this image of living water from the Old Testament (see Jer 2:5, 13; 17:13; Is 55:1).

Question 4. Jesus' knowledge of the woman's past is another example of Jesus' supernatural insight into certain facts about people. Other examples: Jesus "saw" Nathanael under a fig tree (Jn 1:48); Jesus knew the identity of his betrayer (Jn 6:70); Jesus knew that his friend Lazarus had died (Jn 11:14); Jesus predicted Peter's three denials (Jn 13:38). Jesus brings up the woman's past to demonstrate that he was more than just a Jewish stranger and to make her need of a life transformation more obvious.

Question 5. The proper place to worship was another issue that separated Jews and Samaritans. Because the Jews in Jerusalem refused to let the Samaritans worship at the temple in Jerusalem, the Samaritans built their own temple on Mount Gerizim ("this mountain" in verse 20). The Jews promptly tore down the rival, apostate temple, but worship on Mount Gerizim continued. The hatred between Jews and Samaritans would be resolved only in God's new society—the church (see Acts 8:14-17).

Question 8. When Jesus told his disciples, "Open your eyes and look at the fields! They are ripe for harvest" (v. 35), he may have been pointing to the approaching crowd of Samaritans (vv. 39-40). Farmers may have to wait for a harvest after planting seed, but in the spiritual realm (at least on this occasion) no waiting period was required. The harvest is now. In the same way, Jesus sends us into the world to reap a harvest of those who will come to believe in him.

Question 9. This man was probably a Gentile officer in the service of Herod Antipas, the tetrarch of Galilee from 4 B.C. to 39 A.D. Rather than traveling to Capernaum where the sick child was, Jesus heals the boy long distance. John seems to select the most difficult of Jesus' miracles to highlight in his Gospel.

Study 5. John 5. Deity on Trial.
Purpose: To understand that those who reject Jesus as the Son of God do so because of their deliberate denial of convincing evidence.
General note. In the first four chapters of John's Gospel the people tended to respond to Jesus in belief. Beginning in chapter 5, however, a significant change takes place in their attitude toward him. Now his miracles no longer produce belief; they generate controversy, particularly among the Jewish leaders of Jesus' day. Jesus challenged their rigid traditions and their burdensome legalistic rules—and it got him in a lot of trouble.
Question 2. Some manuscripts of the New Testament include a section between verses 3 and 5 about the "moving of the waters" in the pool of Bethesda. (See footnote in the NIV.) It is generally agreed that these verses were not part of the original text of John's Gospel, but they do reflect some of the superstition that surrounded the pool. The people believed that the water in the pool moved because an angel was stirring it. They also believed that whoever stepped in the water first after it moved would be healed. The paralyzed man was bitter because no one would help him get to the water first. Someone always beat him to it. The reality was that the water in the pool was moved by the periodic surge from an underground spring (Morris, *Gospel According to John*, p. 302).
Question 3. The Pharisees of Jesus' day had made sabbath (seventh day) observance the greatest of the Ten Commandments. They believed that they had to build a hedge of protection around the commandment by enacting dozens of lesser laws designed to define exactly what could and could not be done on the sabbath. When Jesus commanded the man to carry the mat he sat on, the only thing the Pharisees saw was Jesus instructing him to work on the sabbath and to break God's command.

The Pharisees were one sect within Judaism. They were committed to absolute obedience to the law of Moses. In their zeal to keep the law, they went far beyond the intention of the law by adding a great burden of regulations on top of the law. The Pharisees were the chief critics of Jesus' ministry.
Question 5. Jesus equates his own work with the Father's work. In effect, he was claiming to do God's work. Furthermore, Jesus called God his own Father. Essentially Jesus was claiming to be of the same nature as God the Father. Jesus' opponents understood exactly what Jesus was say-

ing—he was claiming equality with God.

Question 6. During his life on earth, Jesus lived in dependence on the Father. Nothing Jesus did came from his own power; he acted in the Father's power. The Father repeatedly expressed his love for Jesus and has entrusted the Son with incredible privileges.

Question 8. Encourage discussion about the validity and weight of the testimony of each witness. Consider why Jesus singled out these particular witnesses.

Question 9. The Pharisees who challenged Jesus were particularly proud of their knowledge of the minutest detail of Scripture and their strict adherence to the law of Moses. Jesus uses the very things they boasted in to bring condemnation to them. These religious leaders had missed the whole point of God's truth!

Question 10. Try to focus the discussion on the personal pursuit of freedom in Christ and a growing relationship with God rather than just avoiding certain churches or more legalistic traditions.

Study 6. John 6. Jesus, the Bread of Life.

Purpose: To awaken in us a new awareness of Jesus' ability and willingness to meet our needs.

Question 1. This miracle is commonly referred to as "the feeding of the five thousand." John does say in verse 10 that "the men sat down, about five thousand of them." Matthew in his account says that the figure did not include women and children (Mt 14:21). Many scholars estimate the size of the crowd to have been around fifteen thousand.

Question 2. Mention to the group the way that Jesus used real-life problems to build faith in his disciples. Apply that to the specific life settings of those in your group. How can we use life's problems to challenge those we are seeking to disciple (for example, children or new leaders)?

Question 4. The Lord may put you in a difficult situation to see if you will trust him or if you will trust your own wisdom and resources. Focus not so much on the details of the problem but on how God may be at work in the person.

Question 6. Jesus tries to focus the people on the eternal satisfaction of a spiritual relationship with God rather than the temporary satisfaction of a physical meal.

Question 8. Equate the words "he who comes to me" and "he who believes in me" (v. 35) with the words "eat the flesh of the Son of Man and drink his blood" (v. 53).

Some Christians think Jesus' statement about "eating [his] flesh" and "drinking [his] blood" refers to the Communion service, the Lord's Supper. On the basis of this passage they believe that eating the bread (Jesus' body) and drinking the wine (Jesus' blood) are essential elements in salvation.

It seems better to understand Jesus' statement as a figure of speech, picturing belief in him as the source of spiritual life. Just as we eat bread and drink water to sustain physical life, so we receive Christ to sustain spiritual life.

Study 7. John 7:1-52. Confused over Christ.

Purpose: To demonstrate how we can respond in a Christlike manner to those who attack our faith in Jesus.

Question 1. Jesus' "brothers" are most likely his half-brothers. Jesus was born only of Mary; these brothers are later children of Mary and Joseph. Four brothers of Jesus are mentioned by name in the Gospels—James, Joseph, Simon and Judas (Mt 13:55; Mk 6:3). Jesus also had at least two half-sisters who are not named (Mt 13:56; Mk 6:3). Some Christians believe Jesus' "brothers" were cousins or even Joseph's children by an earlier marriage. John specifically says that Jesus' brothers did not believe in him. Their comments to Jesus were made in sarcastic tones.

Most New Testament scholars believe that at least two brothers ultimately came to faith in Jesus. James became the leader of the Jerusalem church (Acts 15:6, 13) and was probably the author of the New Testament book of James (Jas 1:1). Judas (not to be confused with Judas Iscariot, Jesus' betrayer) is usually identified as the author of the New Testament book of Jude (Jude 1).

Question 2. In some translations verses 6-10 give the impression that Jesus lied to his brothers. He said in verse 8: "I am not going up to this Feast" and then, in verse 10, he goes up in secret. Jesus, however, was not deceiving his brothers. The NIV gives the correct interpretation of Jesus' statement by inserting the word *yet* in verse 8: "I am not yet going up to the Feast."

Question 4. The Feast of Tabernacles (or Booths) was one of the great religious celebrations in Israel. It took place in the fall of the year. For the eight days of the feast, the Jews lived in homemade shelters. They erected the booths on the roofs of their houses or on the slopes of the Mount of Olives. This national camp-out was a reminder of God's provision for Israel during their forty years of wandering in the wilderness under Moses. They had no permanent homes then—just tents. They trusted the Lord for water and food. The feast became a perpetual memorial to God's grace. It was a joyous feast centered on a lot of singing, dancing and rejoicing. There was also a tradition that the Messiah would come during the Feast of Tabernacles. In the middle of the feast (the fourth day) Jesus began to teach in the temple.

Question 6. The phrase "the Spirit had not been given" (v. 39) does not mean that the Spirit was absent. Jesus is referring to the time when the Holy Spirit would be given to his followers in power (see Acts 2). After that momentous day of Pentecost, believers would be aware of the Spirit's presence and ministry in their lives.

Question 9. Jesus responded to each challenge with courage, with a declaration of truth and with a gracious offer to believe in him.

Study 8. John 7:53—8:11. Caught in Adultery.

Purpose: To show Jesus' compassion toward all of us who are guilty of sin.

Background note. In the NIV this section of John's Gospel is separated from the verses preceding and following by solid lines. The verses are missing from most of the earliest Greek manuscripts of the Gospel of John. Most later manuscripts include the verses at this point in the text (although a few insert them at other places in John and a few make them part of Luke's Gospel). While it raises some textual problems, most evangelical scholars agree with Dr. F. F. Bruce, who calls it "a fragment of authentic gospel material not originally included in any of the four Gospels" (Bruce, *The Gospel of John* [Grand Rapids, Mich.: Eerdmans, 1983], p. 413). For a full discussion of the textual problems, see Morris, *Gospel According to John*, pp. 882-84.

Question 4. Several elements of injustice are embedded in this situation. If the woman was caught in the act of adultery, a man had to be present— but no man was brought and accused before Jesus. If these men wanted "justice" carried out, they could have brought the woman to the Jewish council just a short distance away in the temple. The men there would have been happy to condemn her. Adultery is usually a private sin. How did these men "catch" her at just the right time to confront Jesus?

It is obvious that these men were using this woman to trap Jesus. If Jesus had agreed that she should be stoned, he would have immediately lost his reputation with the people as a man of grace. But if Jesus had set her free, he would have set himself in opposition to the law of God.

Question 5. "There is no hint of why or what [Jesus] wrote. . . . A not unlikely suggestion is that He wrote the word He later spoke. In other words His sentence was written as well as pronounced. . . . T. W. Manson is of this opinion. He says, 'The action of Jesus might be explained from the well-known practice in Roman criminal law, whereby the presiding judge first wrote down the sentence and then read it aloud from the written record. . . . Jesus defeats the plotters by going through the form of pronouncing sentence in the best Roman style, but wording it so that it cannot be executed.' An ancient opinion is that Jesus wrote the sins of the woman's accusers (cf. Job 13:26)" (Morris, *Gospel According to John*, p. 888 and note).

Question 7. Jesus consistently demonstrated a remarkable compassion and concern for women. In a culture that viewed women as little more than the husband's servant, Jesus empowered women to be courageous believers.

Question 8. Forgiveness does not grant the person permission to return to or to continue in sinful behavior. Forgiveness gives the person freedom to change without the threat of punishment hanging over him or her. Jesus was not condoning the woman's sin; he was empowering her to change.

Study 9. John 8:12-59. Shine, Jesus, Shine.

Purpose: To demonstrate how the claims of Jesus divide people according to the response of their hearts.

Question 1. The events of this chapter took place in the treasury area of the temple in Jerusalem (v. 20). Jesus spoke at the end of Israel's Feast of Tabernacles (7:14). During that feast, large menorahs (lamp stands) were set up in the treasury area and were lit at night. It was against the backdrop of those menorahs that Jesus made his claim to be "the light of the world." The visual imagery was striking.

Question 4. Contemporary culture takes a very broad view of spirituality and personal freedom. To tell a person that he or she is wrong in what they believe is the height of social incorrectness. Jesus, however, made the choices very clear. Those who believe in him have life; those who do not believe do not have the life or light of God.

Question 5. It is not completely clear who speaks to Jesus in verse 33. Perhaps those who professed belief in Jesus suddenly find themselves challenging Jesus because their faith is shallow and untested. Their prior claims of belief in Jesus are not supported by what they say now. Their statement that they as Jews "had never been slaves of anyone" was a major-league lie.

Question 6. Jesus charges that, contrary to their claim to have *Abraham* as their father, by their sinful actions these people demonstrate that *Satan* is their spiritual father.

Question 8. By their reaction it is clear that the Jews understood the phrase "I am" (v. 58) to be a claim to deity. The Lord had spoken this name to Moses from the burning bush (Ex 3:13-15). The law's punishment for blasphemy was stoning.

Question 9. The passage shows that a person's opposition to the gospel message is not usually based on rational objections or on intellectual arguments. At the root of a person's rejection of Christ is moral rebellion, a willful assertion of human autonomy that prefers life without God to life under God's authority.

Study 10. John 9. A Blind Man Sees the Light.

Purpose: To encourage us to do the will of God, even when we risk opposition and misunderstanding.

Question 1. Jesus' answer to the disciples' question reveals that God takes full responsibility for the way he has made us. There are no mistakes in God's sovereign plan (see Ex 4:11; Eph 1:11).

Jesus' remark that "neither this man nor his parents sinned" does not mean, of course, that they were sinless. He meant that the man's blindness was not the direct result of anyone's specific sin. The disciples had been taught that tragedy at birth was the direct result of the child's sin before birth. The evidence of the child's sin was the fact that the child kicked in the mother's womb!

Question 4. There is no final answer to this question. Perhaps Jesus was using it as the means of awakening faith in the blind man's heart.

Question 6. The Pharisees had already decided that Jesus could not be the Messiah. They denied that possibility on the basis of Jesus' questionable origin and the fact that Jesus was obviously a law-breaker. When the Pharisees can no longer deny the reality of the miracle, they resort to character attacks and threats.

Question 9. The blind man makes remarkable progress in his understanding of who Jesus is. First he calls Jesus a prophet (v. 17); then he debates the Pharisees' claim that Jesus is a sinner (v. 25); then he asks whether the Pharisees also want to become disciples of Jesus (implying that he had become one himself; v. 27). Finally, when Jesus asks him if he believes in him, the once-blind man answers "Lord, I believe" and worships Jesus (v. 38).

Study 11. John 10. Listening for the Shepherd's Voice.

Purpose: To provide us with strong assurance of Christ's love for us.

Background note. John 10:1-18 is a continuation of Jesus' answer to the Pharisees who challenged him in chapter 9. Jesus explains the character of the relationship between himself and those who genuinely believe in him.

The cultural background of this chapter is extremely significant for a proper understanding of its teaching. A first-century Palestinian shepherd raised sheep primarily for their wool. A shepherd lived with his sheep. He knew his sheep; he named his sheep. Every village had a communal sheepfold with only one door for the protection of the sheep at night. The shepherds took turns guarding the door. In the morning each shepherd would come to the sheepfold and "call" his sheep. He made his own unique sound, a clucking noise or a whistle. Only the shepherd's own sheep would recognize that sound and follow him.

Question 1. Jesus used the familiar picture of the shepherd and his sheep to convey a greater truth. John does not record any of Jesus' parables, which were so characteristic of Jesus' teaching ministry, but John does record some of the allegories that Jesus used. Another example is the allegory of the vine and the branches in chapter 15. In an allegory a common experience or object is used to convey spiritual truth. Jesus used the allegory of the sheepfold to picture our salvation and the intimacy of our relationship to the Savior.

Question 3. The "flock" under Jesus' care would eventually reach beyond the Jewish people to include the whole world. Every Christian is part of Christ's flock (or Christ' body, to use a different New Testament metaphor). Ask the group to focus on the common bonds that link them with other Christians, not doctrinal or denominational divisions.

Question 4. Jesus repeatedly assures us in John's Gospel that his sacrifice is voluntary and not coerced. Jesus joyfully, willingly does what pleases the Father.

Question 5. Between verses 21 and 22 of John 10, there is a time change. The events recorded in John 7:1—10:21 all occur within a few days during and after the Jewish Feast of Tabernacles. That feast was held in late September or October. In verse 22 of John 10 the scene shifts to the Feast of Dedication (Hanukkah). That feast was observed in December. So between verse 21 and verse 22 about ten weeks have passed in silence as far as John's record is concerned, but Jesus' message is on the same theme. He continues to talk about his sheep and about who he is in relation to the sheep.

Question 6. The mark of a true sheep is that he or she responds to Jesus' voice in faith and then follows him.

Question 8. Jesus' argument can be explained like this: In the Scriptures God says to some human beings, "You are gods." The reference is to

Psalm 82:6, where God refers to his representatives in Israel. No one could dispute the fact that God did say that, because the Scriptures cannot be broken. They are the final authority.

If the Scriptures used the word *gods* to refer to persons who simply represented God, how much more appropriate was it for Jesus to call himself the Son of God, especially since he had given them abundant proof of his deity? But they refused to believe.

Question 10. Jesus' assurance of salvation in this passage cannot be disconnected from our responsibility to believe and follow Christ. Assurance comes from the promises of Scripture, from the inner witness of the Spirit and from the witness of a changed life.

Study 12. John 11. Back from the Dead!

Purpose: To be encouraged by Jesus' ultimate victory over death and his power to bring glory out of apparent tragedy.

Question 1. Mary, Martha and Lazarus were siblings who lived together in the village of Bethany. Jesus often stayed as a guest at their home (see Lk 10:38-42). Later Mary would anoint Jesus as an act of devotion (Jn 12:1-11).

Question 2. The common belief in Jesus' day was that the spirit left the body three days after death. Jesus waited until the fourth day so this miracle would seem even "harder." Jesus knew that Lazarus's sickness would not end finally in death, but he delayed in order to display God's power and glory.

Lazarus was revived back to life but ultimately died again. His reviving was different from Jesus' resurrection (and our future resurrection). In the resurrection our bodies will be glorified and we will never die.

Question 3. Martha believes that Jesus could have kept her brother from dying. She also believes in the future resurrection of the body. What Martha does not grasp is Jesus' power and willingness to restore her brother to life now.

Question 4. Jesus' statement could be paraphrased "He who believes in me will have a new kind of life, eternal life, even though he dies physically; and whoever has eternal life and believes in me will never die the ultimate death, eternal death."

Question 5. Real death, according to Jesus, is not what we see at the end of our life on earth. Physical death is simply the transition from earthly life to future life. Real death is separation from God forever.

Question 6. Jesus was moved to tears by the pain and separation that death brings. Death came into the human race as one of the consequences of sin. Jesus came to defeat that enemy, but he is brokenhearted over the pain death brings to a world he loves.

Question 7. Some Christians think that if we grieve over the death of another Christian, we demonstrate a lack of faith in the reality and joy of heaven. But Jesus expressed sorrow because of death. Paul says that we are not to grieve as if we have no hope beyond the grave, but we do grieve (1 Thess 4:13).

Question 9. Miracles alone will not bring people to faith. The authenticity of Jesus' miracles was rarely questioned. Instead his enemies questioned the source of Jesus' power. Jesus said that at the future judgment some people will claim to have performed miracles in Jesus' name but he will disown them (Mt 7:22-23).

Question 10. God's delays in our lives are not final. He will intervene in his own way and in his own time. From our perspective God usually comes to us later than we think he should; from his perspective he comes right on time.

Study 13. John 12. The King's Last Acts.

Purpose: To show us the value of seeking God's will and God's glory even if it means dying to our own desires and goals.

Question 2. The three Gospel writers who record Mary's anointing of Jesus (Matthew, Mark and John) tell us that the perfume was very costly. Ointments and perfumes like nard were imported from India and Arabia and were often purchased as investments. Judas accurately calculated the value of Mary's gift as equal to one year's wages. This pound of nard (or spike nard) may have been Mary's inheritance from her parents. But in comparison to her gratitude for raising Lazarus and her love for Jesus, her gift represented a very small sacrifice. Anointing was an act of worship and an expression of complete devotion.

Question 3. If we are honest, some of us would have been just as shocked as Judas was. Extravagant demonstrations of devotion to Christ will not usually be greeted with applause. More often they will be questioned and rebuked.

Question 4. The popular expectation among the Jewish people was that the Messiah would bring political deliverance to Israel and overthrow the oppressive Roman rulers. Jesus came to Israel with spiritual demands and a kingdom of justice and peace.

Question 7. Jesus saw his death as the means by which his glory would be publicly displayed. He would die, but from his death something wonderfully new would emerge. Furthermore, Jesus would begin to draw all kinds of people into his kingdom. When Jesus says that he "will draw all men" to himself (v. 32), he does not mean that all people will be saved. He means that all kinds of people will come to faith in him—not just Jews but Gentiles too. This would have been particularly meaningful to these Greeks who had come to speak to Jesus.

PART 2: JESUS, THE LIVING WAY TO GOD.

Study 14. John 13:1-17. The Son as a Slave.

Purpose: To impress us with Jesus' example of loving servanthood and to motivate us to display the same spirit.

Question 1. These verses set the scene for Jesus' entire farewell message to his disciples. Jesus knew that the hour had come for the completion of his mission on earth. In that light he wanted to demonstrate the full range of his love for his disciples.

Question 2. The famous portrayals of the Last Supper by artists are almost all incorrect. Jesus and his disciples were not sitting on chairs at a table. They were reclining on low couches arranged (most likely) around low tables in a "U" shape. Jesus, as the guest of honor, reclined in the center position. John reclined on Jesus' right; Judas reclined on Jesus' left. Both men had places of honor next to Jesus, places Jesus had invited them to occupy.

Question 3. When people entered a house, it was customary to wash their feet. A water pot stood outside the door, and usually a slave was stationed there to perform the task. Often the job was given to a disabled or retarded slave who couldn't do anything else. If there was no slave at the door, one of the members of the group would wash the feet of the others out of courtesy. But on the day Jesus and his disciples came to the upper room, no one volunteered.

The "upper room" was a large room in a house that was used for large family gatherings. It was probably built as a second story over the family dwelling below. Visitors had access by way of an outside staircase. Jesus and his disciples had borrowed the room of a friend for this last "family" gathering before Jesus' death.

Question 7. Peter's unwillingness to have his feet washed was a response that characterized Jesus' enemies. But the other extreme ("wash me all over") missed the point too. Peter did not need to be rebathed (reborn); he needed only a cleansing from daily sin.

Question 8. Some Christians regularly practice footwashing as part of their worship. Other Christians do not because the practice is never commanded to the church in the later New Testament. Certainly the spirit of servanthood is to characterize every Christian's life. If your group is open to the idea, you may want to conclude your study time with your own footwashing service. Provide basins of water and towels, and have each person rinse the feet of the person next to them. Usually words of encouragement and love are spoken after each person's feet are washed. It can be a very moving experience but also one that stretches some people beyond their comfort zone.

Study 15. John 13:18-38. A Traitor? Not Me!

Purpose: To teach us to look beyond surface appearance to genuine character when choosing our spiritual heroes.

Question 2. Judas' impending betrayal came as no surprise to Jesus (see Jn 6:66-71). Jesus knew Judas' intention, of course, and yet Jesus continued to minister to Judas in exactly the same way he ministered to his other disciples. No one knew from Jesus' attitude that Judas was the betrayer.

Judas reclined at Jesus' left; John reclined at Jesus' right. John could easily lean back on Jesus and engage in intimate conversation that the other disciples may not have heard or understood. Jesus could also talk quietly with Judas without attracting undue attention. To dip bread in a dish of chopped fruit and give it to another person at the table was an act of friendship. It is comparable to proposing a toast in our culture. Jesus used the gesture to continue to reach out to Judas in love.

You may also want to discuss the statement in verse 27: "Satan entered into him." Judas is the only person described in Scripture as being personally indwelt by Satan. Consider why John would make this point.

Question 5. The new covenant that Jesus made with his disciples had just one commandment (not ten commandments like the old covenant). Jesus' command was to love each other—to make a choice to act for the good of your brothers and sisters in Christ, to love them regardless of their response to you, to keep on loving even when they are unlovely or unlovable.

Question 7. Love is to be the mark of Jesus' disciples. When people around see the sacrificial love we have for each other, they will immediately recognize that we follow Jesus. Compare that quality with other qualities that Christians sometimes think will gain the world's attention—knowledge or miraculous works or political influence.

Question 8. Peter speaks from an exaggerated confidence in his own ability. Peter would follow Jesus in death later on (see Jn 21:19), but Peter wanted to follow Jesus *now*.

Study 16. John 14. Comfort for a Troubled Heart.
Purpose: To understand and claim the comfort available to us in Christ and in his promises.
Question 1. Jesus had revealed that one of his disciples would betray him, that he would be leaving and the disciples could not follow, and that Peter would disown Jesus that very night—troubling words!
Question 3. Thomas and Philip had not fully grasped the fact that Jesus was God in visible form.
Question 4. Those who think Christians are "too narrow" in their belief that Jesus is the only way to God need to be reminded that we are only agreeing with what Jesus himself said. It should also be noted that Jesus did not say, "The church is the way," or "Christianity is the way." He said, "*I* am the way."
Question 5. This chapter contains the first of several sections in John's Gospel on the ministry of the Holy Spirit. If you are unfamiliar with the teaching of the New Testament on the Spirit and his work, it would be profitable to do some reading in a theological work that addresses this important area.
Question 7. Our obedience to Christ emerges from our love for him. We are not motivated to obey Christ by the law (I *must* do this); we are motivated by love (I *want* to do this).
Question 8. The peace Jesus brings is an inner work of the Holy Spirit. It is not dependent on outside circumstances or events. Jesus' peace is a sense of security and safety in his love. The world's peace is simply the absence of conflict. A person of the world can have an abundance of wealth and be in turmoil; a Christian can be in a prison cell or a hospital bed and be at peace.

Study 17. John 15:1-11. The Secret of the Vine.
Purpose: To challenge us to seek a deeper level of commitment to spiritual intimacy with the Lord Jesus.
Question 1. The vine is used in the Old Testament as a figure for the people of Israel as God's chosen people (see Ps 80:8-19). But the psalmist also foresees the coming of a divine Redeemer—"the man at your right hand, the son of man you have raised up for yourself." Jesus was the *true* vine, the unfailing channel of God's grace and power.
Question 2. This is a good place in the study to insert the necessity of being a "branch" (a Christian). No one shares in Christ's life unless there is a faith relationship to Jesus.
Question 3. *Remain* means to be joined to and to stay in that relationship.

By remaining in the vine, the branch draws its nourishment and life from the vine. Believers who remain in union with Christ learn to draw their strength, spiritual resources, life and joy from him. Jesus is talking about more than a casual, once-a-week relationship; he's talking about an ongoing, deepening relationship.

Question 4. Several elements maintain our relationship with Christ: prayer, reading and meditating on the Word, worship alone and in community, obedience to the Spirit, a joyful desire to grow.

Question 5. Fruit in the New Testament is the observable evidence of our true inner nature. If we are branches connected to Jesus the vine, we should demonstrate Christlike qualities in our lives. Paul calls those outward qualities the "fruit of the Spirit" (Gal 5:22-23).

Question 6. A number of views exist on what it means for a branch to be "cut off." One is that the Christian who refuses to grow and bear fruit makes a choice to reject his or her place in Christ. A second view is that this is a reference to God's discipline in the life of an unproductive Christian. The genuine believer does not become separated from Christ but is reproved by God. A third view is that the unproductive branches were not genuine believers in the first place.

If a number of views are represented by members of your study group, give time for a presentation of each view, but don't let this issue overshadow the rest of the biblical teaching. If everyone in the group seems to hold to one view, you may want to challenge that view to test the depth of conviction in the other members.

Question 8. The Holy Spirit will continue to testify to who Jesus was and to what Jesus accomplished. The disciples will also bear that responsibility as eyewitnesses of Jesus' life, death and resurrection. These two sources provide the testimony that still persuades people today to believe on Jesus—the testimony of the New Testament and the inner convincing power of the Holy Spirit.

Study 18. John 15:12—16:4. The Cost of Friendship.

Purpose: To explore the personal relationship that Jesus desires to have with us and to use that relationship as a model for our relationships with others.

Question 2. We use the term *friend* in a much more casual way than the people in Jesus' day used it. For them, friendship included loyalty, equality, the sharing of possessions and even the sharing of secrets. The word Jesus uses here in Greek means someone who is part of the king's inner circle.

Question 5. Jesus had been (and would continue to be) the target of hostility. Once Jesus was off the scene, however, the world's hatred would be directed toward his followers. The response of the unbelieving world to Christians mirrors their response to Jesus.

Question 6. The hostility of the world is the price the believer pays for friendship with Christ. You need to draw the distinction between persecution for Christ's sake or persecution that comes because we do something personally offensive.

Question 7. Jesus had given his generation enough evidence to prove his claim to be God. They heard his words and saw his miracles, but they rejected him anyway. Therefore, they were guilty of rejecting God and had no excuse for their sin.

Study 19. John 16:5-15. Secrets of the Spirit.

Purpose: To realize the power of the Holy Spirit that is available to us as we face the struggles and problems of life.

Question 2. The Counselor mentioned in verse 7 is obviously the Holy Spirit (see 15:26; 16:13-15).

Verse 5 seems to be a contradiction. Someone *did* ask Jesus where he was going. Back in John 13:36, Peter said, "Lord, where are you going?" Peter, however, was not concerned about Jesus' destination but about being separated from him. Instead of rejoicing because Jesus was going to the Father, he was sorrowful about being left alone.

Question 3. The Holy Spirit is fully present in every true believer in Christ. On earth Jesus limited himself to a human body and could only be at one place at any one time. Every believer has personal, direct access to God through the Holy Spirit. If Jesus were here, we would have to wait in line to have personal, direct access to God.

Question 4. The Spirit's work toward the world is to "convict" the world of several important things. The word translated "convict" means to present evidence so as to convince. Those who hear the gospel are convinced by the Holy Spirit of certain facts about themselves and about Jesus. Even those who reject the gospel are convinced of its truth. Their rejection is a matter of the will. They deliberately choose to reject what they have been convinced is true.

Question 6. Jesus' death on the cross and his resurrection from the dead sealed Satan's ultimate condemnation. Satan is still active in our world, but he is a defeated enemy.

Question 8. God has given Christians the responsibility of communicating the gospel message. It is the Holy Spirit's responsibility to convince those who hear the message of its truth.

Question 9. The end result of the Spirit's work of communication to the disciples is the written New Testament. The apostles' written testimony about Jesus is the foundation on which we rest our faith (see Eph 2:19-20).

Question 10. The Spirit is not revealing new Scripture to us today. His ministry is to illumine our minds to understand what is already written and to apply that truth to our contemporary culture.

Study 20. John 16:16-33. Peace in a Time of Trouble.

Purpose: To equip us to handle crisis situations for which we have no explanation or answers.

General note. This section is especially conducive to open sharing of struggles, fears and failures. You may not have answers to the problems that emerge from the group. The focus of the study is that, even in the times of greatest darkness and confusion, we have not been abandoned. We can still cling to the Father's love and the Spirit's presence. It might be profitable to end the study with specific prayer for the people and the needs in the group.

Question 1. The disciples were confused by the prospect of Jesus' departure and then return—and by the timing of those events. They had already heard some very disturbing things and now Jesus adds more to be concerned about.

Question 3. We have questions: What is going on? Why is this happening? When will it end? When they go unanswered, we can be certain that God is at work and will ultimately bring joy out of a difficult and desperate situation.

Question 5. The disciples would find new confidence in prayer. They could now come to the Father in Jesus' name—in his place, in his authority. Whenever we pray for what Jesus would pray for in the same situation, the Father will give it to us. The question "What would Jesus do?" has been overworked, but maybe we need to ask "What would Jesus pray for?"

Question 7. As the disciples hid in fear after Jesus' crucifixion, they must have thought back often to Jesus' assurance of the Father's love.

Question 8. We don't find peace in sin or disobedience, but after we return to the Lord we find peace in his forgiveness and love.

Study 21. John 17. Jesus Prays for Us.

Purpose: To reveal the concerns of Jesus' heart as he faced the cross and to see how those concerns should be our concerns as his followers.

Question 1. Jesus' primary goal in coming to earth was not directed at human beings but at God the Father. He came to reveal how good and gracious the Father is to provide a way for disobedient humanity to be restored to a right relationship with him. This is a theme all through John's Gospel. Jesus came to do the Father's will (4:34; 5:30, 38; 6:38-39) and the Father's work (5:36; 9:4). He also came to speak the Father's words (3:34; 7:16; 12:49), to bear witness to the Father (5:36; 7:28) and to live in a close relationship with the Father (8:16, 18, 29; 16:32). Christians are to follow Jesus' example in pursuing God's glory (17:18; 20:21).

Question 3. The phrase "eternal life" refers to a kind of life, not just a length of time. Eternal life begins when a person enters a relationship with God through faith in Jesus Christ (Jn 3:36; 5:24). At that moment we have a whole new kind of life—God's life, eternal life.

Question 5. The crucifixion and death of Jesus would look for a while like Jesus' defeat and Satan's victory. The enemy would use that time of confusion to push the disciples toward despair, disbelief or even suicide. Jesus asked the Father to protect the disciples during that particularly vulnerable time. A follow-up question might be, "Is that the kind of protection we can still ask God for?"

Question 6. The word *sanctify* means to set apart. In Scripture it has a double thrust—to be set apart from sin and to be set apart for God's use. Explore both themes in your discussion.

Question 7. The tendency is to read organizational unity into Jesus' prayer instead of organic unity. It might be profitable to review the "unity" pictures Jesus has already used: one flock (Jn 10) and Jesus as the vine and believers as the branches (Jn 15).

Study 22. John 18:1-27. Trial & Trust.

Purpose: To show Jesus' sovereign control and calm confidence in a time of trial, and to give us assurance in our difficult times.

Question 1. The obvious emotion is fear. But explore other struggles the disciples must have faced. What would they have felt toward Judas? What about their promises to die with Jesus?

Question 2. Jesus wanted to make it easy for Judas to find him and for the soldiers to arrest him without incident. The olive grove was also a place where the disciples could escape easily into the night. John portrays Jesus always as the victor, never as the victim. Jesus orchestrates the whole scene.

Question 3. Jesus spoke a simple word of response: "I am." That was the name the Lord spoke to Moses from the burning bush in Exodus 3:14. Jesus attributed to himself the personal name of the Lord God.

Question 4. Jesus establishes that the soldiers are seeking only him, yet Peter steps outside Jesus' protection in a feeble attempt to fight off the entire group. Our attempts at working things out sometimes complicate what God has already planned and put into place for our good.

Question 6. Peter realized the seriousness of Jesus' situation. Another cross could quickly be found for him! Despite his noble intentions, Peter's faith was too weak to stand up to this challenge at this point in his life.

It might be helpful to outline the main events of Jesus' trials in sequence for the group. A study Bible or a book on the life of Christ should provide you with those details.

Two men are called the "high priest" in John 18—Caiaphas in verse 12 and Annas in verse 19. Annas was the legitimate high priest of Israel under Jewish law. Some years earlier, however, the Roman authorities decided to sell the office to the highest bidder. Annas proceeded to buy the position for a whole succession of men. Caiaphas, the high priest that year, was Annas's son-in-law. Because Annas was the real power behind the office, the Jewish leaders took Jesus to Annas first.

The other disciple mentioned in verse 15 has generally been identified as John, the author of this Gospel. John may have been from a priestly family and would, therefore, have been known to the high priest.

Question 8. Peter probably entered the temple complex thinking he would try to get close to Jesus and somehow set him free. What Peter wasn't expecting was a challenge from a servant girl. Once in the "denial" mode, it became more and more difficult to admit his true allegiance.

Question 10. The suggestions shared in answer to this question need to be "tested" by the response of others in the group. Sometimes our attempts to "stand for Christ" are really expressions of pride or self-righteousness. How did Jesus act in front of others when he was questioned?

Study 23. John 18:28—19:16. Character Test.

Purpose: To demonstrate that even though Jesus was crucified unjustly, he willingly submitted to death for our sins.

General note. Pontius Pilate was a Roman career bureaucrat about the same age as Jesus. His official title was procurator of Judea. He came to Judea in A.D. 26, hoping that he would soon be promoted to a more civilized section of the empire. From the moment he arrived in Judea, however, everything went wrong. After two or three major political blunders,

Pilate found himself at the mercy of the Jewish leaders. They knew that enough pressure would make Pilate do whatever they asked.

Jesus' final religious trial had been held in the temple area in the chamber of the Sanhedrin (san-heed-rin), the Jewish supreme court. Right next to the temple was the Roman fortress of Antonia. The Roman army was stationed there, and Pilate, the governor, lived there. So it required just a short walk to bring Jesus to the civil authority for final condemnation.

Question 2. While about to execute an innocent man, the Jewish leaders are scrupulously concerned about avoiding ceremonial contamination during Passover. They refuse to enter Pilate's house for fear of coming in contact with something or someone unclean.

Since the Sanhedrin, the Jewish council, did not have the authority legally to impose the death sentence, they needed the sanction of Rome to have Jesus executed. John also recognizes that a Roman style of death was necessary so that Jesus' words about the manner of his death (being "lifted up") would be fulfilled (v. 32). The penalty under Jewish law for blasphemy was stoning.

Question 3. Jesus' kingdom did not originate within the world system. Its principles of operation are very different from the kingdom Pilate represented. You may want to discuss some of the differences.

Question 4. Pilate repeatedly said that he found nothing in Jesus' actions or words that warranted death. Pilate tried to play on Jesus' popularity with the crowd to get Jesus released, but to Pilate's shock the crowd called for Barabbas to be released, not Jesus. Then Pilate tried sympathy. Jesus was whipped and presented back to the crowd. But they still called for his death.

The flogging mentioned in 19:1 was no light punishment. The whip had pieces of metal or glass embedded in the leather thongs. The beating ripped open the flesh not only on a person's back but also on his chest and face. Jesus would have been almost unrecognizable after the ordeal.

Question 7. Roman mythology was full of characters born from a union of the gods with mortals. Was Jesus a son of one of the gods? The thought brought panic to Pilate's pagan mind.

Question 8. Isaiah, the Old Testament prophet, said that the Messiah would face execution as a "lamb to the slaughter" (Is 53:7-8). Jesus spoke to Pilate only to confront Pilate with his own need and the injustice of his condemnation. Later church historians claim that Pilate eventually committed suicide after being recalled to Rome and exiled to Gaul (modern France).

Question 9. Try to get beyond the superficial responses and help those in the group realize that we probably would have caved in to political pressure just like Pilate did.

Study 24. John 19:17-42. Obedient to Death.

Purpose: To grasp the incredible price Jesus paid for our redemption from sin.

Question 1. A fascinating article on the crucifixion of Jesus was published in 1986 by a medical doctor, a pastor and a graphic artist. If you wish to obtain a copy for your own research or for the group, the article is titled "On the Physical Death of Jesus Christ" by William D. Edwards, Wesley Gabel and Floyd Hosmer, *The Journal of the American Medical Association* 255 (March 21, 1986): 1455-63.

Question 4. Very few of Jesus' followers were brave enough to identify with him at his execution. John mentions only five: Jesus' mother, Mary; his aunt, Salome, the mother of John (who wrote this Gospel); Mary, the wife of Clopas; Mary Magdalene; and John, the author. Although Jesus was occupied with the most important event in the history of redemption, he remembered to care for the needs of his mother. Usually younger brothers were entrusted with a widowed mother's care but Jesus' brothers at this point were not believers. Jesus placed Mary in the care of his cousin, John.

Question 6. Jesus spoke on seven occasions during the six hours on the cross. John records three incidents. His cry, "It is finished," was a declaration of victory; the full payment for our sins had been made. The word Jesus spoke in Greek meant a debt had been paid in full. Nothing else needs to be or can be added to our redemption. Those who believe in Jesus are under no further obligation before God. We walk in obedience to God out of love for him and out of gratitude for what he has done, not because we add anything to our salvation by good works.

Question 7. The bodies of crucified criminals were normally thrown down the side of Golgotha into the valley of Hinnom, Jerusalem's garbage dump, where they were devoured by scavenging animals. Joseph of Arimathea and Nicodemus (the same man we met in Jn 3) had enough clout and money to get permission to take Jesus' body and bury it. A few of Jesus' followers washed his body and quickly wrapped it with strips of linen held in place by gummy spices. Since the next day was a special holy day for the Jews, no bodies were left hanging on crosses overnight.

Now or Later. John had to verify Jesus' actual death in order to substantiate a genuine resurrection in chapter 20. Every witness affirmed that

Jesus was dead—John himself (v. 26), the executioners and Jesus' friends who took his body away.

The legs of the victim were broken in order to speed his death. Survival on the cross required the victim to push up with his legs so that his lungs could fill with air. Hanging from his hands produced paralysis in the diaphragm. Only the constant and painful up-and-down movement allowed the man to live. When his legs were broken, he could no longer push up and, as a result, died in a few minutes. A victim of crucifixion did not die from loss of blood but from suffocation.

The blood and water that flowed from the spear wound in Jesus' side (v. 34) was another evidence of his death. The blood in the heart had already separated. The heavier red blood cells had separated from the plasma, the clear liquid John called "water." John records this observation as another proof that Jesus actually died. Modern theories that Jesus swooned or fainted on the cross and later revived have no support in the facts recorded for us by eyewitnesses.

Study 25. John 20. The Son Is Up!

Purpose: To affirm the reality of the resurrection of Jesus, and to show how we can respond to people who doubt or disbelieve.

Question 1. The position of the burial wrappings (vv. 6-7) is a significant piece of evidence. Jewish burial practice involved wrapping the washed body in strips of linen from the shoulders to the toes. As the wrapping was done, a mixture of gummy spices was spread on the cloth to hold the binding and to cover the stench of decay. A large square of linen cloth was wrapped over the head and face and was tied under the jaw.

When Peter and John entered the tomb, they saw the linen burial cocoon still in place, but the body was gone. The cloth that had been around Jesus' head was in its place by itself. The resurrection body of Jesus had passed through the burial wrappings, and they had collapsed in place.

Question 2. Jesus' resurrection was not just a "spiritual" experience in which Jesus continued to live on in the hearts of the disciples. The New Testament eyewitness writers unanimously affirm that the very tomb in which Jesus had been buried was empty a few days later. The women had not gone to the wrong tomb and been mistaken in their assumption. Jesus had risen bodily from the dead.

Question 3. The second line of defense for Jesus' resurrection is his appearances to many people in different places and circumstances at different times.

Question 4. Jesus gives his disciples proof of his resurrection by showing them his hands and side. He pronounces his peace on them (a gift he had promised before his death). Jesus also gives them the Holy Spirit (v. 22). The Holy Spirit would come upon the disciples in power seven weeks later at the Feast of Pentecost (see Acts 2), but this empowerment would carry the disciples through the weeks ahead.

Question 5. Thomas could not be classified as an easily persuaded disciple who was caught up in some vague hope that Jesus had come back to life. Thomas had to be persuaded with undeniable proof.

Question 7. Jesus left Thomas with his doubts and questions for a whole week before he intervened. Sometimes it is best to leave the doubter in his or her struggle for a while. We think we have to provide all the answers to the skeptic immediately, instead of letting God work.

Question 8. Christians are persuaded today to believe in the resurrection by two factors: the clear testimony of Scripture and the inner witness of the Holy Spirit. Both are essential. It is not enough to believe the *fact* of the resurrection. We must receive the risen Christ into our lives and hearts.

Question 9. The message of the gospel is not only that Jesus died on the cross for our sins. The other essential element of the gospel is that Jesus rose from the dead. His resurrection proves that his claims are true and that his sacrifice was acceptable to the Father (read 1 Cor 15:1-8).

Study 26. John 21. A Walk with a Resurrected Man.
Purpose: To demonstrate Christ's ability to use us for his glory, no matter what our past failures have been.

Question 1. Some interpreters think that Peter and his friends were just taking some time off. Others see Peter's return to fishing as a return to his old way of life before he left everything to follow Jesus.

Question 3. In spite of his failure and his denial of Jesus, Peter still loved Jesus and wanted to be near him.

Question 5. It is not immediately apparent in most English translations, but in the Greek text of this passage, Jesus uses different words translated *love*. Jesus asks Peter twice, "Do you truly love me?" (vv. 15-16). In his question Jesus uses the verb *agapao*. In his response, "Yes, Lord, you know that I love you," Peter uses the verb *phileo*. The third time Jesus asks the question, he too uses the verb *phileo*.

While some scholars hold that these two verbs are essentially synonymous in this passage, a case can be made that the change is intentional and significant. Those who hold the change to be significant stress the uniquely Christian use of *agapao*, "to choose to love and to commit oneself sacrificially to the person loved."

Phileo, on the other hand, is generally used of love between friends and relatives; it stresses love based on relationship and emotional attachment.

If we accept that the difference is significant, then it appears that even though Peter's love was not all that Christ wanted it to be, Jesus was still willing to use Peter in ministry, saying, "Take care of my sheep."

Question 6. Genuine repentance is marked by humility and renewed love for Christ. Peter was no longer making the boastful statements he had made earlier. A new spirit of honesty is reflected in his words. Jesus, however, does not put Peter on probation. He gives him kingdom work to do.

Question 7. Perhaps Jesus began discussing death to keep Peter from being overly confident about his loyalty to Christ in the future. He also gave Peter assurance that even his death was under Christ's control.

We are never told in the Bible about Peter's death, but several early Christian writers give us the details. Peter was arrested at the order of the Roman emperor, Nero. When he was taken to be crucified, Peter asked to be crucified upside down. He did not consider himself worthy to die in the same manner as his Master. His request was granted.

Question 9. We will give an account of our lives to God, not to other people. That doesn't mean we ride roughshod over other people's lives, but ultimately we are responsible to please only one person, Jesus.

Douglas Connelly is senior pastor at Parkside Community Church in Sterling Heights, Michigan. A writer and speaker, Connelly has written Bible studies and books, including The Bible for Blockheads *and* The Book of Revelation for Blockheads *(both Zondervan).*

Other LifeGuide Bible Studies by Douglas Connelly

Angels
Daniel
Elijah
Encountering Jesus
Forgiveness
Good & Evil
Heaven
I AM
The Lord's Prayer
Meeting the Spirit
Miracles

What Should We Study Next?

A good place to continue your study of Scripture would be with a book study. You might prefer to try a shorter letter. *Philippians* (9 studies by Donald Baker), *Ephesians* (11 studies by Andrew T. and Phyllis J. Le Peau) and *1 & 2 Timothy and Titus* (11 studies by Pete Sommer) are good options. If you want to vary your reading with an Old Testament book, consider *Ecclesiastes* (12 studies by Bill and Teresa Syrios) for a challenging and exciting study.

There are a number of interesting topical LifeGuide studies as well. Here are some options for filling three or four quarters of a year:

Basic Discipleship
Christian Beliefs, 12 studies by Stephen D. Eyre
Christian Character, 12 studies by Andrea Sterk & Peter Scazzero
Christian Disciplines, 12 studies by Andrea Sterk & Peter Scazzero
Evangelism, 12 studies by Rebecca Pippert & Ruth Siemens

Building Community
Christian Community, 10 studies by Rob Suggs
Fruit of the Spirit, 9 studies by Hazel Offner
Spiritual Gifts, 12 studies by Charles & Anne Hummel

Character Studies
David, 12 studies by Jack Kuhatschek
New Testament Characters, 12 studies by Carolyn Nystrom
Old Testament Characters, 12 studies by Peter Scazzero
Women of the Old Testament, 12 studies by Gladys Hunt

The Trinity
Meeting God, 12 studies by J. I. Packer
Meeting Jesus, 13 studies by Leighton Ford
Meeting the Spirit, 12 studies by Douglas Connelly